DEAR
ANNE AND NAN

DEAR
ANNE AND NAN

ANNE B. ADAMS
AND
NANCY NASH-CUMMINGS

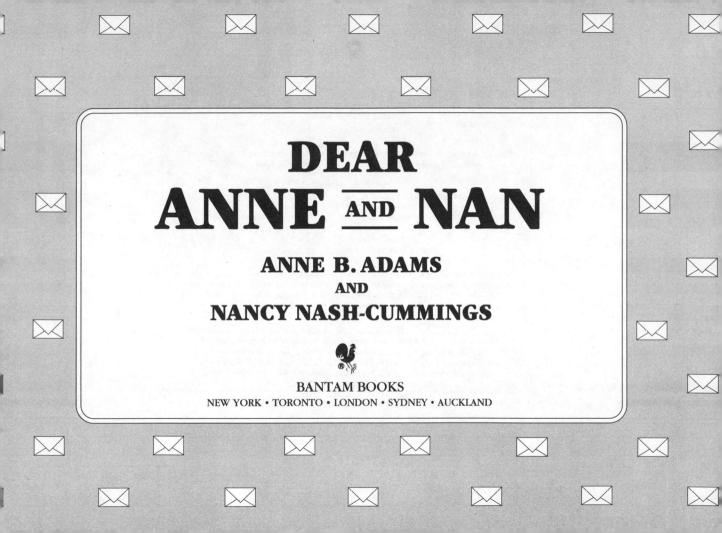

BANTAM BOOKS

NEW YORK • TORONTO • LONDON • SYDNEY • AUCKLAND

DEAR ANNE AND NAN
A Bantam Book/May 1992

Dedicated with love
to our parents

To Nan's mother, Nancy Van Slyke Nash,
and to the memory of her father,
Edgar Vanderhoef Nash.
To Anne's mother, Ruth Potter Duell,
and to her father,
Frederick Baldwin Adams.

ACKNOWLEDGMENTS

Although it is impossible to list the names of the hundreds of readers and friends who have helped us and written us over the past eight years, here are a few of the people and organizations whose tireless efforts on our behalf have made this book (and our column) possible.

Frank Teagle, citizen and epistler extraordinaire
Dan Woodbury and all the other fine folks at Whetstone Press
University of Vermont Extension Service
Robert Blay, record collector and music expert
Lyle Rice and Richard Seitler, antique musical instrument resources
Meredith Wright, fabric conservator and historian
Karen at Pegton's Yardstick
Pat Baril, restaurateur and food expert
Norm Patch at Ascutney Antiques and General Store
All our helpful friends at the Vermont Country Store in Weston
The Vermont staff of Senator Patrick Leahy's office
Morton ("the Factotum") Stillings, fixer of anything and everything
Jack Woolley, our electrical engineer
Richard Kirschner, conservator, Shelburne Museum, Burlington, Vermont

Richard and Jane Adelson, antiquarian booksellers
Sanford Stele, who introduced us to Bantam
Barbara Woodbury, faithful correspondent and fount of information
Vinnie Penna, our tireless, diminutive eighty-year-old contributor to the column
The wonderful staff at the Norman Williams Public Library, Woodstock
The Research Staff at Howe Library in Hanover, New Hampshire
Bill and Louise Borger of Authorized Appliance in Rutland
Johnnie Francis, the Northern Blue Mountain Yodeler of Rutland, who knows (and remembers) hundreds of old songs and poems

and all our readers and correspondents

TABLE OF CONTENTS

DEAR ANNE AND NAN -

WHO ARE ANNE AND NAN?

In late summer of 1982, at a dinner party given by a mutual friend, Anne and Nan were introduced and then seated across the table from each other. In short order, we established the following: Although Anne was born in New York City and Nan in Minneapolis, we both had spent time in Cambridge, Massachusetts, and in the suburbs of Detroit. We had shared an obstetrician and had both tried valiantly (and unsuccessfully) during the course of nine months of visits to make him laugh. Both of us, with a sigh of relief, had moved to Vermont in the 1960s, each bringing with her two young children. (Nan subsequently had a third.) We both had been divorced, though Nan had subsequently remarried. We both had worked in the private and not-for-profit sectors and, having been brought up in families that placed emphasis on "one's debt to society," had given time to the performance of "good works." We also discovered that we were both relentlessly inquisitive about anything and everything, had flypaper minds, and, perhaps as a result of years at camp, boarding school, and institutions of higher learning, loved to get mail.

We never spoke to another person during the entire dinner party except to say, "Please pass the salt."

As time went on we found further similarities. We are both voracious readers and like many of the same books, though Nan tends to read what Anne refers to as "hard" books, like explications of Jungian theory, while Anne tends more toward biographies, novels, and downright trash. We love to garden (and both have greenhouses), watch anything that flickers, coffee thick as sludge, and asking questions. We hate housework and shopping for food but love to cook . . . as long as we don't have to do it every day.

Our differences are few but deep. Nan is a compulsive fitness addict. Anne, on the other hand, thinks exercise is an invention of the devil. Nan has closets full of fashionable clothing, some dating from college days. Anne generally dresses as if she had just been outfitted by the Salvation Army, and frequently has. Nan prefers watching videos in the evening; Anne watches at 5 A.M. Anne is devoted to cats and dogs; Nan is devoted to dogs, chickens, and Sid and Nancy, her two finches.

Anne has worked as a free-lance writer and for many years was director of two centers for multihandicapped children. Nan began working as a stringer for Vermont's *Rutland Herald* in 1973 and went on to start a weekly newspaper. This past year we both have taken a "sabbatical" in order to work on this book and get ready for the weddings of our two daughters, who managed to choose, much to our dismay, exactly the same date for their ceremonies.

Since the publication of our first book in 1989, we have found we have yet another thing in common: we love going out on the lecture circuit, or, as we have come to call it, "The Anne and Nan Road Show." We think that, having both come from large and extended families, and having both been regarded as the family clown, our appetite for an expanded arena of performance was developed at an early age.

Finally, we share a dream, which is that someday we will have a real office (we both work at home under frequently chaotic conditions) with real desks, a copier, a fax machine, an 800 number, file cabinets to hold our papers (which at the moment are stuffed into paper bags and cardboard boxes), and a strict (though kindly), highly organized Mary Poppins sort of person to help us take care of all the above.

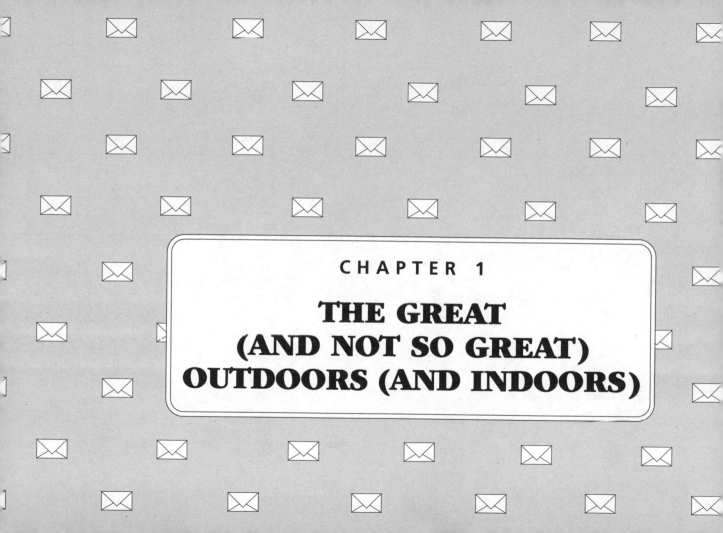

CHAPTER 1

THE GREAT
(AND NOT SO GREAT)
OUTDOORS (AND INDOORS)

HOW DOES YOUR GARDEN GROW?

The answer is, some years are better than others. Anne once lost her vegetable garden to a herd of ravenous deer; Nancy to a mysterious appearance of fusarium wilt. Mice have eaten our spring bulbs (moles, contrary to popular belief, make the tunnels the mice use but do not eat the bulbs themselves: their mouths are too small). Aphids eat our dahlias; white flies and potato bugs chew and suck away cheek by jowl with tarnished plant bugs; Japanese beetles establish populous colonies on the canes of our raspberries. On a perpetual picnic, slugs and cutworms munch on snacks of broccoli and cauliflower. But no matter how bad the pests may be, gardening in Vermont, where the weather is described as being eleven months of winter and one month of mud, is a challenge and, given the short growing season, generally rewarding. Whatever grows, grows quickly and luxuriantly. Particularly zucchini.

Question:
"Why do Vermonters lock the trunks of their cars in August?"

Answer:
"So people can't leave zucchinis in them."

LIGHTWEIGHT ROTOTILLER

Q Does anyone make a small, lightweight rotary cultivator? We want to start a garden (hopefully next year) but it won't be very large so we don't want a big machine, but something handy and easily portable. Any ideas?

A.B.
Ascutney, Vermont

A Absolutely! As the result of a Reader Feedback letter to Anne and Nan, we discovered that there was just such a machine as you describe above. We sent for the info on it and it sounded perfect for our needs, so we ordered one. Our Mantis Tiller/Cultivator arrived a couple of days later, and has proved to be the best gardening investment we've ever made. It weighs only 20 pounds (tines, motor, and all) and yet does such a great job that we were able to sell our large Rototiller, hang up our shovels, and rusticate our hoes. It tills, weeds, furrows, mixes in compost, and with the addition of a couple of attachments, aerates and dethatches the lawn and edges the garden beds.

You can write for a free brochure to Mantis Manufacturing Company, 1458 County Line Road, Department 775, Huntingdon Valley, PA 19006, or you can order the tiller through a catalogue available (free) from Gardener's Supply, 128 Intervale Road, Burlington, VT 05401. If you are going to put in a garden, the above catalogue is invaluable: Gardener's Supply is one of the largest mail-order suppliers of organic and environmentally sensitive gardening products in the U.S.

Tomato- and Pepper-Planting

When transplanting your tomatoes, mix a teaspoon of Epsom salts in with the dirt at the bottom of the hole, then fertilize once a month as usual. Peppers love phosphorus as much as tomatoes love magnesium: bury a book of matches alongside each of your pepper plants at transplanting time and watch them grow!

HOMEMADE FERTILIZER

Q Is there a chance you might have the recipe for fertilizer that you talked about on the radio last week?

A.O.
West Lebanon, New Hampshire

A Here it is. To 1 gallon of water, add 1 teaspoon saltpeter (available at your drugstore), 1 teaspoon Epsom salts, 1 teaspoon baking powder, and ½ teaspoon household ammonia. We figured out what all these ingredients represent if translated into the chemical compounds listed on packages of commercial fertilizer and came up with the following: saltpeter provides potassium and nitrogen, Epsom salts provides magnesium, baking powder adjusts the pH and provides phosphates, and ammonia provides nitrogen. The problem with this recipe is that it does not provide the essential trace minerals available in commercially packaged plant fertilizer, such as copper, iron, and zinc. However, don't despair! The addition of 1 teaspoon of liquid seaweed (available in most feed and garden stores and plant nurseries) will do the trick.

VEGETABLES IN CRISIS

Q Help! It's only the second week in June and many of the plants in my vegetable garden are dying. Everything looked great for a few days after I put in the young plants. Now several tomato, zinnia, and basil plants are dying. First the leaves turn brown on the edge, some have curled up while others are mottled and have teeny holes in them. I change the location of my tomatoes each year and have sprayed them with pyrethrum and they continue to look very sad. I've been told the disease is in my soil, that it's called leaf blight, and I need to change the location of my garden. Is there anything I can do this year?

E.M.C.
Windsor, Vermont

A Chances are that your young plants are suffering from a condition called "shock." This occurs when, after transplanting, there is a dry spell which the root development of the seedlings isn't well established enough to withstand. Unable to draw sufficient moisture from the soil to nourish its foliage, the leaves of the plant wilt and curl. A few good doses of water, either rain or hose, will revive your plants and they will sprout new leaves to replace the old. "Shock" can also occur in more well established plants, again if there is a prolonged dry period. It is particularly prevalent among tomatoes, which, if not watered, will lose most of their foliage. However, if they have already set their fruit, your harvest will not be affected. The "teeny holes" are probably made by flea beetles. These are rarely troublesome enough to warrant spraying.

TRANSPLANTING

Q My husband and I have just finished building a new house and are starting to landscape around it. A friend of ours has offered us as many daylilies as we want: is it all right to dig them up and transplant them now? Also, there is a huge field of lupine growing down the road from us and I'd like to dig some of that and transplant it too.

L.N.
Hartford, Vermont

A As far as we are concerned, daylilies are virtually indestructible: if your friend runs out, we'll be happy to give you some of ours! There's no reason why you shouldn't be able to transplant them at any time. Dig up the plants, wrap them in wet newspaper, bring them home, dig some holes, and throw them in. Water well. The best time to transplant anything in the North Country, from June through August, is in the evening. As for lupine, we suggest that you gather the seedpods rather than dig up the plants. In the early spring, when the frost is out of the ground, broadcast the seed where you wish the lupine to grow, and rake lightly into the soil.

There's an interesting story about the fields of lupine one sees by roadsides in northern New England. In the 1920s, an Englishwoman who summered in Maine grew some lupine in her flower garden. It flourished so well that she collected the seeds and when she went on walks, or was riding in her car, she would stop and broadcast handfuls of seed into a field or onto a roadside bank. She would then collect seeds from the lupine that grew up as a result of her efforts and would give them to her friends so that they, too, could sow the roadsides with flowers. She came to be known in Maine as the Lupine Lady. A wonderful children's book has been published about her: it is called *Miss Rumphius*, written and illustrated by Barbara Cooney.

HOLLYHOCKS

Q I am writing for information on hollyhocks. I planted some out in front of my house and they have taken over the flower bed and drawn a swarm of bees. I am allergic to bee stings and am writing to see if you can give me some advice on how to get rid of the hollyhocks. I have tried everything I can think of, but they keep coming up and spreading. Any information you can supply on how to get rid of them once and for all will be deeply appreciated and save me from living in fear of getting stung.

G.H.
North Clarendon, Vermont

A As with most plants, if you want to get rid of them, you can't, and if you want to grow them, same thing. We're afraid you're going to have to put up with one more summer of fear and trembling. Hollyhocks are biennials and self-sow in the fall, so you currently have two generations of hollyhocks in your garden. However, once your plants have finished flowering this summer, let the flowers die off and cut off the seedpods while they are still green. This will not only prevent the hollyhocks from self-sowing, but will weaken the plant—it will not be able to survive the winter. As to your problems with bees, Nan's husband says he never gets stung, nor does his crew of carpenters. "My great-aunt told me this," he said. "If you get attacked by wasps or hornets or bees, just move slowly and say, really fast, over and over again, 'Bread and butter, bread and butter, bread and butter.' I don't know why it works, but it seems to every time."

Yellow Jacket and Wasp Stings

For fast relief from agony and pain, apply a poultice of water and meat tenderizer! We think this works because the papaya in the tenderizer "melts" the insect's stinger.

SOWING

▽△▽

Q This year I ordered a lot of seeds from gardening catalogues to start indoors. Some of the seeds, especially the perennials, are so tiny that I found it impossible to sow them by hand. Any suggestions?

E.L.
Montpelier, Vermont

A One solution is to go to your nearest pet store and buy a bag of aquarium sand. Put a small amount in a saltshaker, mix in the seeds, and sprinkle on your prepared seed flat. Cover lightly with potting soil. Solution number two is to mix the seeds with the contents of a packet of clear gelatin. Add water according to the instructions. As the mixture gels be sure that the seeds are evenly distributed. When gelling is complete, lay spoonfuls of the mixture on the soil in your flat. Cover lightly with more soil. Water well.

IN THE WILD

▽△▽

Q A bit of spring would be welcome, so I'd like to force some forsythia, but I don't know how. Can you help?

BLOOMING
Corinth, Vermont

A Spring-blooming trees and shrubs such as forsythia, crab apple, and Japanese quince that formed their buds last summer will flower indoors. Cut 2- to 3-foot branches and mash the cut ends with a hammer. Place in a bucket of water in a bright, fairly cool (55- to 60-degree) room until the buds begin to open.

Cut Flowers

To prolong the life of your cut flowers, put a dollop of Clorox in your flower water. This keeps the bacteria, which eventually clog the flower stems and cause the blossoms to wilt, from developing. Caution! Do not do this if you are using a silver or pewter vase. It will cause the inside surface to tarnish irrevocably. Instead, add a generous amount of regular (i.e., not diet) ginger ale.

Q I love milkweed blossoms and long to use them as cut flowers, but they always go limp on me. How can I prevent this?

K.D.
Cambridge, Vermont

A When you cut milkweed, it begins to drool a milky substance. In order to keep the stems from going limp, you need to seal them to keep the milky juices in. The easiest way we know to condition the stems is to sear the cut ends with a kitchen match. An alternative is to put 2 to 3 inches of the stems into simmering water. Hold them on an angle so the steam won't affect the flower heads. Watch the air bubbles as they come from the cut ends and hold the stems in the water until the bubbles stop.

CLOVER

Q We have a small patch of what appears to be white clover at our camp in Groton. These few square feet produce dozens of four- and five-leafed clovers and this year we've even found a seven-leafed stem! Do we have a mutant patch? Is seven leaves record-breaking agriculture? What can you tell us about extra-leaf clover?

A.O.
Montpelier, Vermont

A As it turns out, not a whole lot, although we did discover that the record number of leaves for white clover, as published in the *Guinness Book of World Records*, is fourteen. We got in touch with the New England Wildflower Association in Framingham, Massachusetts, and they said that your patch does, in fact, sound very unusual. When we asked what should be done about this apparent phenomenon, they replied, "Enjoy it!" They added that if you were interested in doing a little experimentation, you could discover if this is a true genetic mutation by attempting to propagate the clover from seed. Clover patches generally propagate through their root clumps, so characteristics of the parent clump will persist.

If it is in fact a true mutation, you could collect the seed, sell it, and get rich! Or something.

WINTERING OVER

Q I was given a small Christmas cactus this year. It's green, but for some reason it doesn't grow and has no blooms. Can you advise me on how to perk it up? It's in potting soil, and I water it occasionally. It's in a 10-inch pot.

MRS. E.A.B.
Wells River, Vermont

A A Christmas cactus is actually not a cactus at all, but a rain forest epiphyte. While a real cactus dislikes having wet feet, the Christmas cactus's soil should be kept moist at all times. It should also be fed once a month with 15-15-15 plant fertilizer. When we researched your question, we were horrified to discover that we have done absolutely everything wrong in encouraging our five-year-old cactus to bloom. According to the literature, the cactus needs about six weeks of cool weather (take it out of your sunny window) and long, continuous absolutely dark periods from mid-October through the first week of December. If the dark period is interrupted, the plant will not set buds. Now we keep our cactus in the greenhouse, where the temperature rarely gets below 65 degrees, move it outside in the summer, never expose it to prolonged periods of darkness . . . and it blooms profusely not once but twice a year and has gotten so large, we are thinking of dividing it.

Q My houseplants spent the summer outside. I brought them in in mid-September and they have become droopier and droopier. I've fed and watered them, and they still look sick. What am I doing wrong?

> SYLVIA
> Mendon, Vermont

A Making the transition from outdoors to in can be hard on houseplants. Often the droopy look is the reaction of the plant to drier and hotter air. Misting daily can help. Also, your plants might have brought some pests inside with them. If there aren't any obvious signs such as spots, specks, or fine webs (a sign of red spider) on the leaves, you should probably check the roots. Take the plants out of their pots and shake the soil from the roots. Wash the roots in a solution of 1 teaspoon of Ivory Soap to 1 quart of water. Repot in fresh soil, using sterilized containers.

Q I have bedded my rosebushes away for the winter. They are floribunda hybrids. Usually I use hay and mulch to cover them, put a bran sack over all this, then cover with plastic bags and tie them down. This year I used rolled-up balls of newspaper and leaves instead of hay and mulch. Do you think the newspaper will affect the roses? The ink, I mean, from the print?

> J.C.B.
> Bradford, Vermont

A The ink from the print is going to be the least of your worries! Using newspaper as mulch is *not* a good idea, according to Leonard Perry, who is the Ornamentals expert at the University of Vermont's Department of Plant and Soil. Newspaper decomposes very quickly and then, like leaves (which he doesn't recommend either) it mats, smothering the root hairs of your rosebushes. He says the best thing for protection is what you used to use: either hay or straw piled about 2 feet deep. Then cover the bush with bird netting . . . or bran bags, if you have them.

GROWING MUSHROOMS

Q Would you please tell me about how to grow organic mushrooms inside year-round. Could you also recommend some informative reading on the subject.

R.P.
Shrewsbury, Vermont

A It would take more space than we have to even begin to tell you how to grow mushrooms. We had always imagined it to be a simple process until we started researching your question: we have learned it is extremely difficult. Not only is preparing the growing medium a laborious process, but so is keeping the right temperature and humidity, propagating the spores, and protecting the mush-rooms from about 1,001 diseases. We suggest you send for the booklet *Mush-*

room Growing, No. A2760, Agricultural Bulletin Building, 1535 Observatory Drive, Madison, WI 53706. The cost is 15 cents; add another 50 cents for postage and handling.

JAPANESE BEETLES

Q They're everywhere! They're everywhere! What can I do about these terrible pests? I even find Japanese beetles in the shoes I leave outside! And please don't tell me in the middle of summer what I should do in the spring. I need help now!

D.C.
Hartland, Vermont

A Oddly enough, a couple of days before we received your letter and its desperate cry for help, we received the following from D.I. of Cherry Hill, New Jersey. "This past weekend Japanese beetles were destroying a new tree I had planted on my landscape. Even though I had two Japanese beetle traps, they were going to town. In a last-ditch effort to save the tree, I sprayed Avon's Skin-So-Soft on the tree and on the grass and bushes surrounding my house. Not a beetle since! It has rained, and the sprinklers have been on, and I have not had to respray!" Okay, D.C.: it's up to you!

POTPOURRI

Q I have fond memories of a cut-glass bowl that my mother had in our parlor that contained dried spices and rose petals. I would like to make one of these with our roses and wonder if anyone has directions.

B.W.B.
Chester, Vermont

A We had a long talk with a friend of ours up north who owns an herb and flower shop, and who makes his own potpourri. Here is how he does it.

To dry: Pick the flowers after the dew has dried but before the sun has become strong. Place no more than ¾ of an inch of flowers or petals in a mesh bag or brown shopping bag with four or five pen holes punched in either side of the bag. Discard all stems and leaves.

Hang in a dark place, as sunlight will bleach out colors. The ideal temperature for drying is between 80 and 90 degrees, so an attic is ideal. If you mix buds in with petals, do so with caution as the bulkier the flower is, the more moisture it contains and the longer it will take to dry.

You can also dry flowers and petals in the oven: one layer per tray. Set oven at 150 degrees and leave the oven door open so that air can circulate. Try to keep light out as much as possible. *Or,* you can use your microwave, but dry only a couple of teaspoonfuls at a time. You'll have to experiment with the settings. The end product, using any of these methods, should be crisp, dry, and free from any moisture. The two things you want to avoid are (1) mold and mildew and (2) fading.

Once all petals, buds, etc., are dry, place in a bowl or glass jar. As you want spice potpourri, add cloves, pieces of *dried* orange peel, and crushed cinnamon sticks "to taste." For a rose or other scented potpourri: Poke a hole in the middle of the mixture and pour in a fixative, either cellulose fibers (crushed corn husks) or orris root. Both of these are available at natural food stores and herb shops. For 1 pound of loose ingredients add 3 or 4 ounces of fixative. Then add fragrant oil to the fixative (½ ounce per pound of flowers). There are a wide range of scents available, again at natural food stores and herb shops, at a wide range of prices. Let sit 20 minutes and mix into flowers.

A COOL DRINK FOR A HOT GARDENER

Q Could you find a recipe for a drink they call Ginger Water? It was used in the hay fields when we were young. It could really quench your thirst.

J.L.F.
East Clarendon, Vermont

A We didn't know what Ginger Water was, but many, many of our readers did and remembered, as did J.L.F., carrying it out to the hay fields in buckets and pitchers to quench the thirst of their parched menfolk. D.T. of East Wallingford wrote,

"Ginger Water is what we always called it, but I understand it is officially known as Switchel. Although I grew up on Ginger Water and prefer it to the more common Gatorade, it is great fun to offer some to the uninitiated. Ginger Water can take some getting used to. At any rate, for 1 gallon:

1½ cups of a blend of maple syrup, brown sugar, and molasses. At least ¼ cup must be molasses.
1 cup cider vinegar, fresh and strong
1 tablespoon fresh ground ginger; more if desired
1 teaspoon salt

Top off with very cold water to make 1 gallon. Shake well.

"This is the classic 'Yankee Haymaker's Drink,' but I have heard that as one travels farther north, a couple of beaten eggs and/or a cup of raw oatmeal may be found in Switchel. Switchel is guaranteed to pull the sweat out of your pores, and, for some, the shoes off your feet. Try some."

PREDATORS, PESTS, AND RELATED PROBLEMS

OUTDOOR MARAUDERS

DEER

Q This spring I planted a number of fruit trees in an old orchard that is pretty far from the house. I'm worried that as winter progresses, the deer are going to come and help themselves to the tender bark of the saplings. Any ideas?

L.D.
Colchester, Vermont

A Wrap the trunks of your young trees with stretchy steel-mesh wrapping (this is available at your local plant nursery), or if you wish to avoid the expense, you can use torn-up bed sheets or old Ace bandages—basically, anything that will cover the bark and still let the tree breathe. To keep the deer from nibbling on the twigs and branches, call around to your local beauty salon and/or barber and ask them to save you a day's worth of hair clippings (or if business is slow, a couple of days' worth). Put the clippings in old nylon stockings (or pantyhose legs) or net bags, and hang one on each tree.

WOODCHUCKS AND MOLES

Q Woodchucks are just ruining my daughter's garden. What can be done other than shoot, trap, or fence?

B.D.
Fairlee, Vermont

A The only option remaining is the use of gas cartridges, available at feed and hardware stores. You drop them into the burrow . . . if you can find it. Neither Anne nor Nan is bothered by woodchucks: first, because we have dogs (geriatric though they may be), and second, because our gardens are fairly close to the house. Nan also fences her garden, but we have heard that woodchucks will not only burrow under fences (unless they are sunk to the depth of 1 to 2 feet) but will climb over them. Over the years, readers have sent us many suggestions and

Moles
Although they leave an unsightly mess, remember that moles are helpful little creatures. They dine primarily on insect grubs, particularly those of the rose chafer and Japanese beetle. They do not dine on bulbs or tubers: their mouths are too small. The culprits are meadow mice who use the mole tunnels as expressways to your garden.

solutions to the woodchuck problem. Drowning, burning, and gassing with carbon monoxide have been among the more draconian solutions; less violent suggestions have been the use of blood meal (very expensive and quite hard to find) and the contents of one's bladder, both liberally sprinkled (although not necessarily simultaneously) around the perimeter of the garden. A friend of ours tried a Hav-A-Heart trap, and after many days of baiting the trap and watching her garden continue to diminish, she managed to catch a baby skunk; the woodchuck obviously preferred unfettered browsing. How about it, readers? Any new ideas?

Two readers wrote with essentially the same solution, and we think it sounds peachy, as it doesn't call for measures that could hurt other wildlife, pets, or children. The letter from A.M. of Williamstown, Vermont, reads, "This is the method my husband uses to get rid of woodchucks and he has got quite a few. Soak a rag in kerosene or No. 2 heating oil (gas is too flammable to use). Let it drip in a safe place away from pets and children. Put the rag in the woodchuck hole and fill the hole with dirt. The stench drives the woodchuck away . . . forever." Finally, a friend of Nan's phoned her from Ohio. "I don't know what all the fuss is about," he said. "Getting rid of woodchucks is easy as pie. Put on a pair of gloves, unwrap a package of Juicy Fruit, and put the unwrapped sticks of gum in the woodchuck hole. Presto! No more wood-chucks!" He wasn't kidding, either.

READER FEEDBACK

Baiting Traps
Whether you are baiting a mouse, rat, or Hav-A-Heart trap, always wear gloves, preferably clean ones. Otherwise, the smell of "human" on the bait will serve as a caution flag to the rodent you are attempting to tempt.

SNAKES

Q I moved into a lovely old farmhouse and had charming stone walls built around the flower gardens that border a busy highway. Much to my squeamish surprise, the next spring when I returned to plant my flowers, etc., I found my walls were infested with millions of snakes. Yikes! I hate snakes and dread thinking about even going near those gardens. Would you or any of your readers know how I can convince my unwanted guests to use some other spot for their snake motel? I am desperate, but would prefer a natural solution versus any type of poison, etc.

J.P.
Chester, Vermont

A Stone walls and snakes, like love and marriage, are just one of those things that go together. The only way you are going to get rid of the snakes is to get rid of the stone walls: this information was given us by both the Vermont Fish and Game

Department and the Extension Service. With the exception of an occasional rattlesnake nesting high on mountain ledges in some parts of Vermont, there are no poisonous snakes around. So while we realize that some people have a deep and abiding aversion to snakes, those in your walls not only are harmless to you but, as insect eaters, are a beneficial addition to your gardens.

PIGEONS

Q What is the best way of keeping pigeons away from bird feeders? We love birds, but hate these flying rats. The town of Springfield has hundreds of them but has done nothing about it!

R.A.
Springfield, Vermont

A The best you can do is to buy a birdseed mixture that does not contain cracked corn, and, as pigeons are essentially ground feeders, have feeders with ledges that are too small to support the alighting pigeons. The kind we recommend as being pigeon-proof and squirrel-proof is the tubular plastic type, supported on a pole. Finally, try to keep the area around your feeder as clean of seed as possible: the tubular feeder, as opposed to the tray type, also discourages the flinging about of seeds that some birds, such as the ravenous grosbeaks, seem to enjoy.

WOODPECKERS

Q A woodpecker has decided that our TV antenna is much better than a tree. The antenna is mounted on a roof above our bedroom and every morning the racket starts at sunrise. The bird alternates between the metal tubing (a metallic, banging noise) and the junction box (a more hollow sound). Turning the antenna with the rotor motor sends the woodpecker away for about 10 minutes. This morning I almost hit it with a rock. Any suggestions other than getting a gun? This woodpecker is driving us crazy!

A.P. and A.D.
Worcester, Vermont

A We can only counsel patience and bet you that by the middle of June, at the latest, the woodpecker (actually, it's probably a yellow-bellied sapsucker), having established territorial rights to his satisfaction, will have ceased and desisted. Don't brain him or shoot him; he chose your antenna because it makes the loudest and most satisfactory sound around: so much better than the dull, pedestrian thunk-thunk of bill against hollow wood. (This spring, Anne had a sapsucker battle raging around her house: one chose the hollow pipe holding up her satellite dish and the other banged away on the TV antenna. For a couple of weeks, it sounded like the Tet offensive was being mounted on her property each dawn.)

Squirrel Invasions

This has been a problem for many of our readers who have trees growing close to and/or overhanging their roofs. The best solution to the problem (other than cutting down the trees) that we received came from W. F. of Barre, Vermont. "First we spread mothballs around the attic and the squirrel family departed whence they came. Then we found the source of entry and plugged same. Since then, no squirrels. They do not like mothballs."

CAT PREDATORS

Q I am a country-dwelling cat lover. I thought living out here away from traffic would increase the life expectancy of my cats, but no! Over the past few years I have lost several cats—they simply vanished without a trace. The most recent disappearance was last week. It's hard to believe they wandered off. My hunch is that some other animal caught them. I have spoken to several people about foxes (I know there are some living nearby) and everyone has a different story. I'm also wondering about those big weasels called fishers, because I've heard they are quite vicious. Please ask your "experts" which wild animals, if any, prey on house cats. I'll bet other people would like to know too.

J.M.
Woodbury, Vermont

A We consulted three "experts": our vet, our resource at the Vermont Institute of Natural Science, and a Fish and Game biologist. The consensus is that a fox is the least likely culprit; they far prefer birds, rodents, and an occasional small rabbit. A fisher, on the other hand, is a good possibility, as is a coyote, a great horned owl, or a neighborhood dog. Cats, if they have been altered, will usually stay within a ¼- to ½-mile radius of their home. If for some reason they are chased or frightened out of that radius, they will be hard-pressed to find their way back. Anne has lost a few cats over the years: she found the regurgitated remains of one under the perch of a great horned owl deep in the woods. Your best bet is to alter your cats and try to keep them in at night.

SKUNK ATTACK

☑☑

Q We're planning a vacation at a camp we've rented in the Adirondacks, and we're going to be taking our dog with us. He's a city dog, and when brains were handed out, he wasn't standing in line. What do we do if he encounters a skunk or a porcupine? We really don't want to have to keep him tied up.

G.R.
Concord, New Hampshire

A Given the fact that your dog is not, let us say, mentally acute, we recommend strongly that you keep him either tied or on a leash, at least until he gets used to the area and has marked out his territory. Otherwise, you may discover that you have a lost pet. When and if you do decide to let him roam free and he encounters Mother Nature in one of her less benevolent moods, we have the following suggestions. If the porcupine quills are just around his muzzle, cut the ends off the quills with a pair of scissors and then pull out each quill with pliers. If he has taken a bite of the porcupine, and the quills are in his mouth and tongue and most likely down his throat as well, you'll have to take him to a veterinarian, who will knock him out and complete the extraction process. The skunk problem is a little simpler. Any solution that contains 5 percent acid, such as tomato juice, white vinegar, or wine (a good thing to know if your dog gets "skunked" while you're on a picnic) should do the trick if applied right away. The acid cuts through the oil in which the skunk scent is suspended. Follow with a good soapy bath. You'll probably want one too.

Recently, we were doing a call-in radio show and got on the subject of skunks. A lady phoned in with the following information: the absolutely best thing to get rid of skunk smell is a liberal application of . . . douche!

READER FEEDBACK

BITERS AND CHEWERS

BLACK FLIES, MOSQUITOES, ETC.

Q I know you've recommended Avon's Skin-So-Soft as a deterrent to black flies and other biting insects, but frankly, I can't stand the smell. Is there anything else I can use now that they have taken a lot of the other effective bug dopes off the market as possible cancer causers?

M.S.
Fairlee, Vermont

A While on a visit to her retired-doctor uncle in Florida, Anne tried out a "bug dope" the good doctor swears by: PreSun 39 Sunscreen. It worked against Florida biters, so she tried it when the black flies appeared with springtime in Vermont. It works here too. A word of caution: some people are allergic or sensitive to the P-aminobenzoic acid (PABA) that is one of PreSun's active ingredients (it's also the ingredient Uncle Bill thinks repels the insects). Try it out first on a small area of your skin and check after 24 hours for any adverse reaction.

BREEDING GROUNDS

Q Every year at about this time, a pond forms under our back porch. By June, it is a perfect breeding ground for mosquitoes. Do you know of anything biodegradable that I could pour into the water to make it hard on mosquito eggs? The space beneath the porch is accessible only through the space between the floorboards that make up the deck. Would Dr. Bronner's liquid biodegradable soap that I've seen in health food stores work on the mosquitoes? Its label lists it as, among other things, a mosquito and black fly repellent.

ERIK
Rutland, Vermont

A Empty a bottle of Joy liquid dishwashing soap through the spaces between the floorboards: it will create a film on the top of the water, depriving the mosquito larvae of oxygen. You probably could also use Dr. Bronner's, but ours is ancient and its label unreadable. You should probably be thinking about a long-term solution to your problem: either putting down drain tile around the perimeter of your deck or removing a few floorboards and pouring sand into the "pond." Replace the floorboards with screws rather than nails, so that you can add more sand as needed.

MOSQUITO REPELLER

Q I am enclosing a clipping from a mail-order book I received recently for a battery-operated mosquito repeller. Do these things work? I would pay twice the price, gladly, if I knew I wouldn't be wasting my money. Also, what about the high-pitched sound it emits? Is that more annoying than the bugs would be?

P.B.
Barre, Vermont

A While we're not sure about the effectiveness of the repeller offered in your catalogue, we are sure that the "high-pitched sound" is ultrasonic, and so wouldn't bother you. In the course of our perpetual and personal war on biting insects, we stumbled upon a repeller that we can promise *does* work against 80 percent of all species of mosquitoes. It can be hung either from your belt or placed near you in the garden or on the patio. Called the Mosquito Hawk, it makes a barely audible clicking sound that mimics the sound of a dragonfly, a mosquito's number one enemy. Battery-operated (and the battery is included!), it costs $12.95 plus shipping, and is available from Gardener's Supply, 128 Intervale Road, Burlington, VT 05401, or call 802-863-1700.

OUTSIDE PESTS MOVE INSIDE

CLUSTER FLIES

Q I remember reading in your column the name of a substance that was supposed to be used in June as a preventive measure against the appearance of those loathsome cluster flies in August, September, and October and maybe even every really warm day during the winter. But I neglected to write it down and so am asking, nay, verily, pleading with you to once again print it. I don't want to spend any more time with nasty cluster flies now that I know there is a specific remedy for their infestation.

B.C.
Wolcott, Vermont

A In fact, there is nothing you need to do in June. By then the cluster flies that have been living in your walls and other nooks and crannies inside the house will have droned their black and hairy way into the great outdoors. There, bothering no one, they will spend the summer laying their eggs (preferably in old manure piles) and drinking fruit and flower nectars. By August, when the nights begin to grow cool, they (or their young) will start coming into your house in search of a warm place to spend the winter months. There is no surefire way, unfortunately, to keep them out entirely, especially if you live in an older home. The flies crawl through the smallest cracks around windows, doors, and eaves to take up residence. On any sunny, warm winter day, thinking it spring, they will awake and swarm to the windows, attempting to make their escape. The best way to discourage them is, in late August, to spray permethrin (Ectiban) on the outside of your house, particularly around eaves and doors, and apply pyrethrum around window frames before installing storm windows.

ANTS

ᗺᗺ

Q Help! We have tiny red ants that are overrunning our kitchen. Ant traps are completely ignored. Any suggestions to get rid of these creatures would be greatly appreciated.

M.C.
East Corinth, Vermont

A Your ants are probably disregarding the ant traps because they are finding whatever they want to eat or drink right in front of them. They may like sweets, starch, grease, crumbs, or just the moisture on your water pipes. We've had all kinds of suggestions as to how to deal with ant infestations, but the consensus is that the first essential step is to discover where they are coming into the house. Then you may do one of several things. Sprinkle their trail with cayenne pepper (one reader sprinkled black pepper around her entire foundation and hasn't had an ant since) or white flour. Draw a chalk line around where they are coming in. Make a spray of 2 tablespoons detergent and 2 tablespoons Epsom salts in 1 gallon of water. Or, as M.L. of Springfield, Vermont, suggests, "Mix 2 cups of Borax with 1 cup sugar. Punch holes in the plastic cover of a coffee can or something similar and use to sprinkle around the *outside* of the house near the foundation."

EARWIGS

▽▽▽

Q We have an infestation of earwigs in our house. We've been spraying with a chemical, but it doesn't seem to be doing the trick and we have two small kids. Do you or any of your readers know how to get rid of them, or at least slow them down?

E.K.
Arlington, Vermont

A A pamphlet on earwigs we obtained from the Vermont Extension Service says, "When the pest invades the home, its objectionable appearance, unpleasant odor, and habit of lurking among foodstuffs and clothing and dropping onto the table, make it a major nuisance.... Their invasion of houses begins some time in July.... If it becomes necessary to spray indoors, use a household spray containing diazinon or malathion: one labeled for indoor use against earwigs. Spot treat along baseboards, drainpipes, and under the edges of carpets. Do not treat furniture or floor areas near where children play." All of which, we realize, doesn't answer your question but is the best we, or the Extension Service, can come up with. Does anyone out there have a home remedy for E.K.?

From D.L. of Chittenden, Vermont: "Loosely cover a tin can with brown paper, grease the inside from the top to about one third of the way down with bacon grease, and fill with water up to the grease. Place the can where you suspect the pests are. They love bacon grease and after feasting, drown. Empty each morning. I trap about 150 with four traps."

READER FEEDBACK

From Mrs. F. in Rutland, Vermont: "I put moth flakes around the outside of the house and I haven't seen an earwig in over a week. I went outside tonight and found a lot of dead earwigs, so I put a second dose of moth flakes around the house and I put mothballs in the cellar."

From W.C. of Londonderry, Vermont: "E.K. of Arlington has my deepest sympathy. I was bothered with the pests for years. I finally found a formula that helped slow them down. Mix 1 tablespoon Ivory dishwashing liquid in warm water, not hot. I use a spray bottle that some other spray liquid came in. Earwigs don't like Ivory liquid for some reason. I carried the spray bottle with me every time I went out or near where earwigs were living and after two or three times of spraying, there seemed to be no more earwigs. The next spring they came back again, but this time only a couple of sprayings got rid of them. Spray under the baseboard on the outside of your house; this helps to keep them out. This year I added a teaspoon of Lysol liquid cleaner and they didn't seem to come back so quickly."

READER FEEDBACK

SPIDERS

Q I work in a dark, somewhat dank basement office, which isn't bad considering there aren't any windows. One of the things I do to keep my sanity is kill those little spiders by shooting rubber bands at them. It's a test of skill, because if you get closer than six inches you risk being splattered by spider parts. I know that the little guys eat the even nastier six-legged devils, and we should think of spiders as our friends. But they do seem to keep coming back to test my aim. Could it be some sort of spider test into adulthood? (Pass through the gauntlet of the humanoid's missile, and you'll be a spider.) Which leads me to my two-part question. How do you get spider parts off a Dacron-cotton blend shirt? And are spiders, like worms and beetles, a source of protein? Could we find a way to raise them and, after a skillful processing operation, use them to relieve world hunger or create a new McDonald's sandwich?

BASEMENT DAVE
Springfield, Vermont

A You've been down there in the dark much too long.

GENERIC BUGS

Q What causes those little bugs that get into flour products in your cupboards? I've cleaned the cupboards and bought new products, but they even get in sealed containers. Is there anything I can do?

C.M.S.
Rutland, Vermont

A We're puzzled as to just what the bugs are. At first we thought C.M.S. had an infestation of mealybugs, but the cleaning of the cupboards and the buying of new products in sealed containers should have taken care of those. Readers, have you any ideas?

A.T. of Rutland, Vermont, writes: "My sister learned that bay leaves discouraged and eradicated the bugs. So now I drop a few bay leaves into every food (flour, dried fruit, cornmeal, etc.) container and I've had no problems for 10 years or so. I wonder if dispersing bay leaves on the shelves themselves would be effective? It's worth a try and is certainly 'natural' control—no chemicals!"

T.O. of Montpelier, Vermont, says she puts bay leaves down wherever bugs congregate—on shelves, in dry ingredients, and even in woolen clothes packed away for the summer.

L.L. of Woodstock, Vermont, writes, "A friend of mine who worked at General Foods told me the eggs are present in the flour when it's produced. In time the eggs hatch, infesting the product, no matter how it's packaged. But freezing flour and flour-containing products before storing will kill the eggs and prevent them from hatching. I now freeze my flour, Bisquick, etc., for two to three days before I store it and haven't had any problems since."

READER FEEDBACK

FLEAS

▽▽

Q Can you tell me how to get rid of fleas in the house?

L.N.B.
Chester, Vermont

A Although there are all kinds of sprays and gases that are commercially available, they also are poisonous and environmentally unsound. Our favorite benign solution to the flea problem came from *Mother Earth News* and is as follows. Fill a flat dish with water and float a few drops of dish detergent on the top. Place one dish on the floor of each flea-infested room, and suspend a light over each dish so that it shines directly onto the water's surface. The fleas, attracted by the light, will jump into the water: if it weren't for the detergent breaking the water's surface tension, the fleas would bounce right off. Keep doing this every night until no more fleas are caught, then keep it up for ten days or so to catch the batches of fleas that will hatch from eggs and larvae already present in the house.

N.L. of Woodstock, Vermont, writes: "When we had a cat and flea problems, we used to place a plate of milk in the infested room at night. Apparently the white of the milk attracted the fleas, for in the morning the tin would be covered with dead fleas and no light had to be left on to make it work."

READER FEEDBACK

Natural Flea Repellent

The best cure for fleas that we know of is Brewer's Yeast Flakes. MRS. C.V.G. told us, "Start the dog out with one level teaspoon. Do this for a week. Put it on the side of the dish or in the food if your dog ignores it. Continue to give ½ teaspoon every other day once the dog stops scratching. Use this for cats too, but rub the yeast into the fur and put the cat out. The cat will clean its coat and acquire a taste for Brewer's yeast. Then put ½ teaspoon on the side of the cat's feeding dish."

Also, a friend of ours reports that since she has been giving her golden retriever one clove of garlic per day, chopped up in his food, he hasn't had a single flea! We tried it with one of our dogs, who would have nothing to do with her garlicky dinner, and are now hiding the garlic in a chunk of liverwurst, which, when hand-fed, goes right down.

NIGHT CRAWLER NIGHTMARE

Q We have a problem that hopefully you can help us with. When we get a lot of rain, we have many night crawlers and worms on our paved driveway. They even crawl in our garage. Do you know of any product that could be put on the edge of the lawn that would prevent them from crawling on the pavement? We're sick of worms. Help!

L.L.
Barre, Vermont

A Anne's sister, who lives in Texas, swears by diatomaceous earth, which consists of microscopic needles of silica. You can purchase it anyplace that carries swimming pool supplies. She sprinkles it on the lawn outside her house ... even on the carpets inside her house. She says this discourages slugs and other soft-bodied creatures outside and cuts down on the ravenous Texas flea population inside. The latter may be wishful thinking on her part, but she swears it's true.

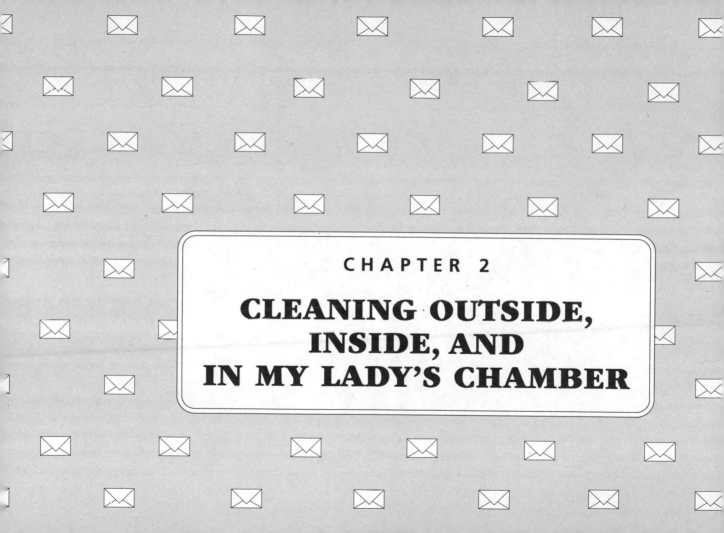

CHAPTER 2

CLEANING OUTSIDE, INSIDE, AND IN MY LADY'S CHAMBER

There are some people who have a natural talent for neatness and order. We have a suspicion that the reason their houses (bathrooms and kitchens in particular) look so clean and organized is because, noticing something that looks dirty, they clean it, and seeing something out of place, they put it away. We, unfortunately, have never mastered the above. It isn't that we don't want to, it's just that our approach to housekeeping is to put things in piles. Until we are unable to make our way to the sink or there are no towels left in the bathroom, picking up, cleaning up, and putting away doesn't seem to occur to us. As a result, we need all the inventiveness we can muster. For example, one day we were sitting in Nan's kitchen, going over our mail. We'd been receiving a great deal of reader feedback about getting the gray out of polyester and polyester-type fabrics. One of the letters read, "Soak the garment in a gallon of hot water to 1 cup of dishwasher detergent, then wash as usual. You'll be amazed at the results!" "Dishwasher detergent!" exclaimed Nan. "If it does such a great job on clothes, why not grease and grime in general?" We filled the kitchen sink with hot water and added a generous amount of detergent. "Let's start with the kerosene lamp chimneys," said Nan. "That will be a real test." We laid them in the water, let them soak a couple of minutes, and when we took them out, they were sparkling clean. Since that historic day, Anne and Nan have used dishwasher detergent for cleaning jobs that go from getting whites whiter than white in a laundry presoak to removing greasy film from kitchen cabinets and fingerprints from woodwork. So does necessity make experimenters of us all! Now, if we could just find a way to reinvent Mary Poppins, we would be set for life.

KITCHEN CLEANUP

BROILER SMOKE

Q We recently purchased an old home, complete with an ancient kitchen. There is no vent or fan over the stove, and whenever I broil anything the kitchen and surrounding rooms get filled with smoke. We can't afford to put in a vent right away. Is there any stopgap measure you can think of?

R.L.
Poultney, Vermont

A Anne had this problem for years (she still can't afford a vent for her stove) and figured it was just one of life's minor irritations. Then a friend suggested that, before broiling, she put ½ inch or so of water in the bottom of the broiling pan, then proceed as usual. It worked like a charm and, since then, broiling has been smoke-free. If you don't feel like washing the pan right away, an added bonus is that as the water in the bottom of the pan cools, the grease floats up and congeals. It can then be skimmed right off. No muss, no fuss.

GAS GRILL GRATES

Q Can I use oven cleaner (spray type) on our gas grill grates which are ceramic-coated cast iron? I have checked my oven cleaner instructions, and it doesn't specify.

AN OUT-OF-TOWN READER
Vernon, Vermont

A Go right ahead and use your oven cleaner. Most stove ovens are ceramic coated, so your gas grill grates will suffer no harm! Just don't use any kind of abrasive scrubber when you wipe the cleaner off.

OVEN CLEANING AND MINERAL DEPOSITS

Q Is there a cleaning strategy for ovens that includes leaving ammonia in a warm oven overnight? What are the details? Will it harm my "continuous clean" surface?

Also, is there a cleaning strategy for an enamel teakettle that has mineral deposits inside?

S.S.
Rutland, Vermont

DEAR ANNE AND NAN -

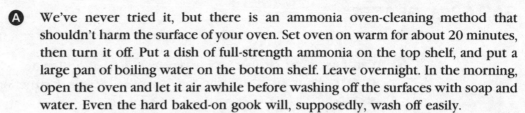 **A** We've never tried it, but there is an ammonia oven-cleaning method that shouldn't harm the surface of your oven. Set oven on warm for about 20 minutes, then turn it off. Put a dish of full-strength ammonia on the top shelf, and put a large pan of boiling water on the bottom shelf. Leave overnight. In the morning, open the oven and let it air awhile before washing off the surfaces with soap and water. Even the hard baked-on gook will, supposedly, wash off easily.

For the mineral deposits in your kettle . . . well, living as we do in hard-water country, there have been many solutions sent in by our readers over the years. Here are but a few. (1) Treat your kettle with a product called Lime-A-Way, available at most hardware stores. Two tablespoons and a bit of a soak should do it. (2) Fill with water to the mineral-deposit line and drop in two or more

More on Hard-Water Scale

If you have a sonic-type humidifier, instead of buying an expensive bottle of humidifier cleaner, just put 2 cups water and 2 cups vinegar in the holding tank. Run it through. For a "jammed" steam iron, fill with white vinegar and set on the Steam setting. Incidentally, do the above two "descalings" outdoors or in a well-ventilated area. Vinegar fumes are very strong. For your automatic coffee brewer, run a 1:1 solution of water and vinegar through it at least once a month. This will insure the proper functioning of the brewer's heating element.

tablets of Polident denture cleaner. Let soak overnight. (3) Boil with a solution of one-half water and one-half 5 percent white vinegar . . . and if you happen to have any marbles, oyster shells, or BB shot around, throw in a handful. Really. The turbulence of the boiling water will bounce these around, and as they bounce, they knock off the loosened mineral scale.

CORNING WARE CLEANUP

Q I have quite a few pieces of the Visions Corning Ware, their amber-colored glassware. I have written to them (the Corning Glass Company) in New York State—no answer. So I am asking you two lovely girls if you know how to clean them. I have scorched some of my pieces. I thought I had tried everything. No luck so far.

D.M.
Springfield, Vermont

A Wish we knew what the "everything" is that you have tried. Anyway, we have had great luck using a *very* strong mixture of dishwasher detergent (such as Calgonite) and hot, hot water. Let soak overnight and then scrub with any kind of plastic-type scrubber.

DEAR ANNE AND NAN -

D.J. of Springfield, Vermont, wrote to let us know that she had called D.M. with the following suggestion: "I use Soft Scrub by Clorox." What a great idea!

D.M. then wrote to let us know that Soft Scrub hadn't worked, as the pots were just too badly scorched. She added, however, that yet another of our readers had gotten in touch with her and suggested she use full-strength oven cleaner! "Worked like a charm," she said. "The pots look like new."

READER FEEDBACK

RUSTY TIN

Q I have a collection of tin kitchen utensils. How can I remove the rust that has appeared on some of them? Also, is there a protective coating I can apply to enhance their appearance and prevent further rusting?

H.C.
Bennington, Vermont

A Use a fine steel-wool pad to clean the rust off your tin utensils. A few drops of white mineral oil or sewing machine oil on the steel wool will make the job easier. If you use the utensils, after each washing coat them with cooking oil to prevent rusting. If they are for show only, you can apply a lacquer called Deft, which comes in a spray or liquid and is available in paint stores. Many of our readers swear by a product called Sani-Wax, which, among its other uses, is both a cleaner and preserver of old tin. Write to Joann Champion, New Horizons, P.O. Box 769, Andover Road, Chester, VT 05143, and she'll send you a price list and a free 1-ounce sample.

MAPLE COUNTERTOPS

▭▭▭

Q We have rock maple countertops, 1½ inches thick, in our kitchen and bathrooms. What do you recommend to clean them? Also, what should be put on to preserve them and keep them looking new?

B.Q.W.
Hartland, Vermont

A Wash them with ordinary soap and water. If they are very dirty, Murphy Oil Soap will clean them up quick as a wink. To preserve them, apply a coat of a carnauba wax such as Minwax Paste Wax or Butcher's Wax (both available at hardware and paint stores). Let stand about an hour, then polish with a soft cloth. An alternative method of cleaning (and one we recommend if you are going to use your kitchen counters for food preparation) is to clean with heated vegetable oil and a soft rag. If the counter is very dirty or stained, use a Teflon pad soaked in the oil and then go over it again with more oil and a soft cloth.

DISHWASHER PROBLEM

ꗑꗑꗑ

Q My dishwasher is ruining my glass and china, leaving what looks like a fine film on it. My instruction manual calls this "etching" but doesn't say what to do about it that I haven't already done. I have a water softener, so my water isn't hard. What can I do before everything is wrecked?

M.V.
Montpelier, Vermont

A At first we thought we could put the blame on your water softener. We suggested it wasn't backwashing properly. A reader let us know we were all wet, and enclosed a printout from a firm called Waterworks in Montpelier, Vermont. It read, in part: "The villain is the excess amount of phosphates in the wash cycle— ironic, because the phosphates are added to the dishwashing compounds to facilitate cleaning." The effect of these phosphates is to chemically soften the water, thereby enhancing the action of the cleaning compound in the detergent. In already softened water, the extra softening increases alkalinity, which in turn causes the etching problem. "When you start with softened water," continued the printout, "you do not need extra phosphate." To ameliorate the problem, only fill your soap dispenser one-half full. As heat acts as a catalyst in the etching process, set the dishwasher thermostat to 140 degrees. This is plenty hot enough to sterilize and provide the grease-cutting action needed for sparkling dishes. Finally, "after washing in phosphate-rich hot water, the outsides of the dishes are not rinsed thoroughly. The blast of heat (often as high as 180 degrees) used in the drying cycle dries out the water droplets left on the glass, concentrating their alkalinity until they leach the heavy metals and silicates out of the dishes. This results in permanent scarring of glass and dinnerware." So use the energy-saving feature on newer dishwashers, which will eliminate the blowing dry of your dishes. Just open the door and allow them to air dry.

DISHWASHER

Q Is it true that a good way to keep your dishwasher flushed out and washing well is to run it through a cycle—water, etc.—without dishes but use a tablespoonful of powdered Tang instead of detergent? Every three weeks or so. . . .

J.B.
Medford, New Jersey

A Strange as it may seem, the answer is yes.

Food Odors

Leave something in your cooler too long? Bad odors in your icebox or freezer? Wipe down the insides with a cloth soaked in vanilla, then leave a saucer filled with instant coffee in the offending space. Although we think baking soda is the best long-term deodorizer, the above works better on short-term terrible smells.

THE BATHROOM

BATHROOM BOWLS

Q How can I clean my toilet bowls? They have a brownish-yellow caked-on crust, probably from minerals in the water (we have a well). Normal toilet cleaners don't seem to do the trick. They look so gross, I am embarrassed. Please help.

J.K.
Plainfield, Vermont

A We received a letter from Milton and Mary Corey of Chester, Vermont, who are distributors of Conklin products. "We have customers from all over the country who use Crust Buster (lime and scale remover) and Rust Off (rust and oxide remover). The powerful formula of these products cleans on the first application and reduces the need for repeat applications, so a little goes a long way. They are both nonabrasive, and so can also be used on Fiberglas, and have a pleasant odor. The Conklin Company tries to make products that will not harm the environment." The information flyer on Crust Buster that the Coreys enclosed says it will "dissolve away hard-water deposits from porcelain toilet bowls." Sounds just the ticket for your problem. The Coreys will be happy to UPS anywhere: write them at R#2, Box 432, Chester, VT 05143. They will send you the Conklin catalogue and a price list. We subsequently received a letter from J.F. of Manchester, Vermont, who wrote: "Your suggestions for lime removal are great, but there is also good old citric acid available at drugstores. I use it for all those greenish deposits."

SHOWER CURTAINS

Q Would you reprint the method for cleaning mildew-stained shower curtains? I have a fabric one that would seem to be beyond hope. I tried washing it with the towels, but that didn't make much difference.

D.D.
Brandon, Vermont

A The shower-curtain-cleaning recipe that we publish at least once a year is for vinyl, rather than fabric shower curtains. (For vinyl: Put your curtain in the washing machine with two towels. Add ½ cup detergent and ½ cup baking soda. Add 1 cup vinegar to the rinse water. Don't spin, but remove immediately and hang.) For fabric, take the curtain outside and brush off excess mildew. Turn your washing machine to the rinse cycle and add one cup Lestoil. Run through rinse cycle once, then wash as usual. If you can, hang the curtain in the sun to dry.

FORMICA

Q The Formica around our bathroom sink looks awful and stained. Can I use bleach on it? Is there anything to make it look better, other than getting new Formica, which, due to the expense, I'd rather not do?

L.G.
Dorset, Vermont

A *Don't use bleach!* You'll take the surface of your Formica right off! First, clean your Formica with a product called Sunny-Side plastic cleaner. This is also good for cleaning and polishing Plexiglas, Lucite, acrylite, and other nonporous plastics. When the Formica is clean, buy an epoxy enamel made by Nybco called Tough As Tile. This can be used to refinish your Formica tops and comes in a variety of colors. (Tough As Tile can also be used to refinish porcelain, enamel, or any other similar surface.) Both these products are available in hardware stores or (usually) from your local Formica dealer.

UPSTAIRS AND DOWNSTAIRS

WALLPAPER CLEANER

~~~~~~

Q Would you tell me where a wallpaper cleaner can be found? It was a doughy substance pink in color and an excellent cleaner. If no longer available, is there any substitute?

M.C.
Fair Haven, Vermont

A We couldn't find your wallpaper cleaner anywhere, which leads us to believe it is no longer being made. It occurs to us that as many wallpapers are now vinyl or vinyl-backed and can be cleaned either with a commercial wallpaper cleaner or with a dilute mixture of detergent and warm water, the demand for the old-fashioned "dough" cleaner is no longer there. As you know, it is unwise to wash really old wallpaper, as the heavy printed paper pasted to the wall will shred. If your wallpaper is old, the best cleaner we can come up with is an art gum eraser, available in art supply stores. Or do what they did in the olden days: clean with a wad of the inside of a loaf of stale bread. However, if the area you wish to clean is a large one, you're in for an arduous task.

DEAR ANNE AND NAN -

R.A. of Rochester, Vermont, and L.K. of East Corinth, Vermont, both sent in the recipe for wallpaper cleaner that M.C. was looking for. Here it is. Take 1⅓ cups flour, 1 cup cold water, 2 tablespoons salt, 2 tablespoons vinegar, 1 tablespoon kerosene, 2 tablespoons ammonia. In a double boiler, mix flour, salt, and water to a smooth paste. Add vinegar, ammonia, and kerosene. Cook, stirring frequently, until the mixture is like a heavy bread dough. Cool. Then knead until elastic and keep in a covered jar. To use: Break off in small portions. Use only downward strokes. Keep turning soiled portion under. Put papers on the floor while using to catch the scrubbings.

READER FEEDBACK

GREASY WALLS

Q Could you give me some suggestions as to how to remove grease from painted walls?

B.J.R.
Windsor, Vermont

A If you want to try a homemade solution for grease removal, combine 1 cup household ammonia, ¼ cup baking soda or Borax, and ½ cup white vinegar. Mix in a bucket with 1 gallon warm water. Always wash walls from the bottom up, as dirty water dripping down the wall can leave streaks that are nearly impossible to remove. By the way, we have found that a coat or two of white shellac right around switchplates on the wall makes that area, which gets the dirtiest, the easiest to clean: dirt, grime, and greasy fingerprints will come off with the quick wipe of a damp sponge.

CLEANING WINDOWS

Q What is the best way for washing windows so they come out clean and streak-free?

P.B.
Barre, Vermont

A There are a number of household solutions. (1) Three tablespoons household ammonia and ¾ cup water. Put the ammonia in a clean spray bottle; add water and a dash of dishwashing detergent. (2) For windows that will purportedly stay cleaner longer, add ¼ cup old-fashioned cornstarch to ½ gallon warm rinse water. (3) For windows in the kitchen that get a greasy film on them (or in rooms where you have a working woodstove), first rub over the glass with a paper towel or old piece of flannel sheeting to remove the dirt, then add a teaspoon of kerosene to either of the above mixtures. Wash and polish.

A Couple of Window-Cleaning Tips

Never wash windows when the sun is shining on them: they'll streak. Use a cheap chamois, old pantyhose, or newspaper to wipe with (no lint left behind). We think newspapers work best. There seems to be something in them that really shines the glass. Use up-and-down strokes on one side of the glass and side-to-side strokes on the other. This way you can see which side needs extra polishing.

MILDEW AND RUST

Q Could you tell me what a good solution is to keep a freezer from mildewing and rusting? It's on a damp cellar floor.

N.L.P.
Proctor, Vermont

A A damp cellar provides the perfect climate for rust and mildew. Our first suggestion is that you get the freezer off the cellar floor—that is, put it up on a wood platform. That will allow the air to circulate beneath it. Second, clean off the freezer surface with straight white vinegar (this will kill the mildew), rinse, and dry with a soft cloth. Then polish with a hard automotive wax, such as Turtle Wax. This will help retard the rusting process.

WHITE RINGS ON WOOD

Q Is there a commercially available product that will take white rings off tables? I know cigarette ash mixed with baby oil is supposed to do it, but neither me or my wife smoke. I've heard that rottenstone powder and oil will also remove the stains, but I'm afraid it may scratch the finish of my table. Any ideas on this?

S.T.
Weston, Vermont

A Our readers wrote us about a product they enthusiastically recommend. It is called Santash and is made by William Farwell of Rutland, Vermont. He sells it by mail order and at craft fairs. We wrote him about his product, and he replied: "We have been in business for over forty years. One of our products is Santash, a liquid that removes white or milky stains from wood, trays, and other pieces. Santash has a special ingredient that does a marvelous job without blemishing the furniture in any way." Santash is available through The Shop of William Farwell, RR #229, Chittenden, VT 05737.

STICKUM

Q A few years ago I moved to a rented apartment with a light beige carpeting that showed every spot. I bought a 9′ × 12′ rug to cover the living room and used double sticky tape to hold the rug in place. When I started to rearrange and move the rug, I found the sticky substance had transferred in bars to the carpeting. Is there anything I can do to remove the sticky bars, other than professional cleaning?

S.R.
Manchester Center, Vermont

A A dry-cleaning solvent will probably do the trick. The problem is that it may also clean the rug where the sticky tape has been, giving the rug a striped appearance. Follow up the cleaning-fluid treatment by rinsing out the solvent with ½ teaspoon of a nonbleaching powdered detergent and 1 pint of water. Rinse again with 1 tablespoon of ammonia in 1 pint water. This rinse is *very* important, because the detergent, if left in the carpet, will act as a magnet for dirt. (By the way, if you go this route, first be sure to test on a small area.)

Q Please, one more time! What is the best way to remove bathtub decals?

M.D.
Northfield, Vermont

A We use nail polish remover. Apply it around the edge of the decals and yank them up. Use more to clean off any remaining residue.

Q Having removed a couple of political stickers from the window of my automobile, I'm left with the remains of glue from the stickers. I've tried everything imaginable to remove what's left, but to no avail. Any suggestions?

E.G.
Montpelier, Vermont

A Lots. (But maybe you've tried them all?) Nail polish remover or straight acetone may work. M. from Springfield, Vermont, wrote us about a product called Thin-O Mineral Spirits. "I use it to remove glue from price tags and labels, using a small paintbrush. It works!" K.H. of Center Rutland, Vermont, uses lighter fluid. He writes: "It does the job exceptionally well. I use Ronsonol but any brand should work as they all contain naptha. Of course, test first on a minor area to determine any adverse effects. It also removes cellophane tape residue." R.A. of Springfield, Vermont, sent us this hint: "After reading an ad for WD-40 (a lubricant you can buy in hardware stores) which recommended using WD-40 for removing price tags, I tried it and it works beautifully!"

To Keep Cast-Iron Sinks, Woodstoves, Etc., Rust-Free
Clean surface, then polish with kerosene and wadded-up newspaper. (*Do not use this on cooking utensils!*)

CLEANING RUSH SEATS

Q The rush seats on our Ethan Allen dining room chairs are very dirty. Is there a way to clean them? I tried an ordinary spray household cleaner on one of them and it was almost a disaster—it swelled and became very rough. I'm baffled and hope you can help.

I.B.
Stratton Mountain, Vermont

A Use a solution of warm water and mild detergent, or even better, a soft soap such as Fels-Naptha. Clean with the above, using a soft-bristle brush; a baby's hairbrush would be perfect. Rinse and let dry. Incidentally, a couple of years ago in researching a question quite similar to yours, we discovered that there are two kinds of rush. One is cane rush, which is either oval or flat and is usually shellacked or varnished when used in furniture making. The other is fiber rush, which we think is what your chair seats are woven from. The latter is actually ground up kraft paper that has been twisted into long strands. It is recognizable, as it is always round.

To Keep Wicker from Becoming Brittle

Hose it down with spray mist from your garden hose two or three times during the summer months.

CLEANING VINYL

Q I have a patio set of a table and four chairs that are of a white plastic type of material. They have become gray in many areas and I have not been able to get the gray off. I tried Comet and Clorox but to no avail. I am wondering if you know of some product that will remove this gray look so that I can once again have a white table and chairs. The legs are metal so I can spray them with white Rust-Oleum to cover the rusted areas (the metal part is not gray, only the plastic) but do not think I could spray the plastic. Any advice or remedies would be welcome.

L.W.
Barre, Vermont

A Trot right down to your nearest automotive store and buy a product for cleaning vinyl car tops—it should do the trick. Also, be sure to use a wire brush to get the rust off the table and chair legs before you paint them. A new product called Simple Green is great for cleaning the filthiest of outdoor furniture, as well as fireplaces, crystal, no-wax floors, etc. It's nontoxic, biodegradable, and we wish we had invented it. It's made by Sunshine Makers of Hunting Harbor, California.

DOGS AND CATS: ODORS AND STAINS

VACUUM CLEANER ODOR

Q Do you have any suggestions as to how I can rid my vacuum cleaner of the doggie odor it emits after a few uses? I have tried commercial rug deodorizing products and baking soda, but the odor eventually emerges. There is a product called Breeze that pops into the vacuum bag. It's fairly effective, but difficult to find. Do you or any of your readers know of a "home remedy" for this problem?

B.C.
Brandon, Vermont

A We called our local Electrolux dealer in Claremont, New Hampshire, who told us about one of their products. It is called Clean Sweep and probably does the same thing as Breeze. This helpful lady said she sometimes used a cotton ball that has been dampened, *not* soaked, with a household soap or cologne—a scent you like. Put the dampened ball into the vacuum cleaner bag and, as the air goes through and out the exhaust, the scent of your favorite soap will waft out.

J.C. of Brandon, Vermont, wrote: "I use a fabric softener sheet which is used for the drying of laundered clothes in the dryer. I prefer the Arm & Hammer brand, but have also used Downy or Snuggles. I find that changing the bag frequently with a new sheet each time works nicely." B.B. of Rutland, Vermont, suggests that B.C. put a few mothballs in the bag each time she changes it. "The musty smell will be gone for good."

READER FEEDBACK

CAT AND DOG URINE STAINS

Q Some time ago, someone wrote you about what to use to remove cat and dog urine stains from hardwood floors. I neglected to save your reply in the column. Would you be so kind as to answer the question again?

BILL
Waterbury, Vermont

A It wasn't Anne and Nan who answered the question, and we certainly wish we knew of a simple solution. The problem with this kind of stain in wood is that the proteins and acid in the urine soak into the wood cells and, depending on the type and finish of the wood, will bleach or discolor them. The only solution we know of is either to scrub the area with a fine steel-wool pad or, if the stain is deep, to sand it. Then apply Minwax Wood Stain in a matching finishing color.

DEAR ANNE AND NAN -

F.P., whose profession is refinishing floors, wrote: "First, sand away old finish on the stains with a 60-grit sandpaper, then bleach out with a solution of oxalic acid crystals (available from your pharmacist). To make the solution: Dissolve the crystals in warm water to the point of saturation. Let stand overnight in a glass jar. Warm mixture again, and apply on stains with a brush. Let dry. Remove residue that remains with a solution of 50 percent white vinegar. Lightly hand-sand with 100-grit sandpaper and reapply whatever finish was on the floor."

READER FEEDBACK

DOG URINE ODOR

Q A while back, you printed the name of a solution that would remove dog urine from wool rugs. I believe the cleaner could be purchased someplace in Maine. Would you mind repeating it? I've misplaced it.

W.K.M.
Chester, Vermont

A We probably get about ten letters a year asking the very question you have asked, and we have yet to come up with an answer that works 100 percent of the time. However, we will give you the benefit of our "expertise" . . . as far as it goes. First, remember that the sooner the urine is mopped up and the rug is washed off, the more likely it is that the smell will not develop. First, mop up the urine with paper towels or a sponge or, best and most absorbent of all, a sanitary napkin. If possible, place napkins below as well as above the stain. Then saturate the spot with a mixture of one-half white vinegar and one-half warm water. Let stand a few minutes, then sop up, again with sanitary napkins, paper towels, or what have you. Finally, spray with Urine Kleen (also known as Urino-clean or Uri-kleen). This is available at most pet supply stores in the East. Otherwise write to G. G. Bean, Box 638, Brunswick, ME 04011. If the odor is an old one, we haven't found anything so far that works to our satisfaction.

J.C. of West Pawlet, Vermont, writes: "You had a letter asking about eliminating urine odor from carpets. I have it! It's in the Grand Union in the air-freshener section. It's called Abolish and says it permanently destroys pet and household odors without leaving any scent of its own. The product is nontoxic and nonflammable. We really had some bad odors in an old house. We sprayed and the odors are gone, gone, gone! It's fantastic." If you can't get Abolish in your neck of the woods, write to Endosome Biological Company, Williamsville, NY 14221.

READER FEEDBACK

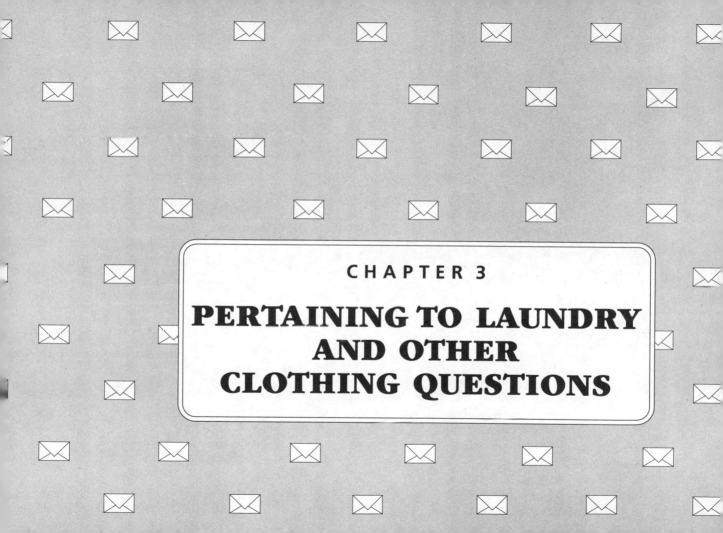

CHAPTER 3

PERTAINING TO LAUNDRY AND OTHER CLOTHING QUESTIONS

To us, the dreariest chores are the ones that are (or at least seem to be) the most frequently required of us: filling up the gas tanks of our cars, replenishing our perpetually empty cupboards, and Doing The Laundry. Nan's husband is in the construction business, Anne's son restores antique racing cars, and both Anne and Nan, if placed in a hermetically sealed and totally sterile environment, would emerge five minutes later, their clothes streaked with soot, spotted with grease, smeared with dirt, and stained, somehow, with spaghetti sauce. Added to the above, our water is so hard that you can bounce rocks off it, which leads to soap scum, yellowing, graying, and clothes that look even worse when they come out of the washing machine than they did when they went in. Over the years, with the help of our readers, we've found some solutions that have eased our burden, but as wonderful and resourceful as our readers are, they have never been able to solve our basic problem: how does one keep one's clothes clean for more than five minutes in the first place?

LAUNDRY

LAUNDRY ODOR

Q Help! Can you tell me why in spite of washing or maybe I'm doing something wrong that our clothes smell as though Fido had been lounging in them? I am wondering what causes laundry to take on such an objectionable odor. I am now using powdered Borax with each load. Are there other remedies?

S.W.
Brandon, Vermont

A We think your problem may be traced to a sock or some other small garment caught either under the spindle of your washing machine (if it's a top loader) or behind the basket (if it's a front loader). If the former, you can lift the spindle right out of the machine yourself and search for the culprit. If the latter, you'll need the help of your local repair person. What happens is that the sock (or whatever) begins to mildew and (ugh) rot; every time you use the machine, the smell of mold and decay gets into your clothes.

Q Could you tell me please if old clothes develop a bad odor even though they are washed regularly? Due to my tight budget, I wear my clothes literally for years and I have blouses, slacks, sweaters, jackets, slips, etc., that have a very unpleasant odor even after they are laundered.

K.B.
Castleton, Vermont

A Manmade fibers such as polyester can develop an unpleasant odor over time, and we are making the assumption that, as your clothes are older, they are made of the above. Here are a few things to try. Add 1 cup of white vinegar or ¼ cup of baking soda to the wash cycle. Washing soda and/or Borax may also help.

Before washing your blouses, sweaters, etc., moisten the underarms with water and rub in a strong antiperspirant soap, such as Dial or Lifebuoy. Or try soaking the clothes for 10 minutes in a mixture of a dollop of Lysol to 1 gallon of hot water, then wash as usual. Finally, if possible, hang your clothes out to dry in the sun; if not, put in the dryer with a sheet of one of the fabric softener/anti–static-cling products sold in your laundry section.

KEEPING WHITES WHITE

Q I have hard water, lots of iron in it, or so I'm told. Every time I buy a white shirt and wash it four or five times, it either turns all dingy yellow or splotchy yellow. I've tried bleach, Tide with bleach, and Spray 'n Wash. Nothing keeps them white or gets them white ever again. Got any ideas? Help!

R.N.
Ludlow, Vermont

A If the iron content of your water is extremely high (your plumber can tell you), you may find that a water softener is a good investment, not only in terms of your laundry but to prolong the "white" life of bathroom and kitchen fixtures as well. Until then, here are some suggestions. You can soak your clothes in Rit Rust Remover, which is available at larger supermarkets and discount stores, or use the old-fashioned method of soaking in water and cream of tartar. Add 4 tablespoons cream of tartar to each pint of water, bring to a boil, and put your shirts in the boiling solution until they turn white. Another old-timer recipe is to mix oxalic acid crystals (available from your pharmacist) in cold water; dip the shirts in and out of the solution until the discoloration has disappeared. Rinse immediately in a bath of cold water to keep the fabric from being harmed. And last but not least, a couple of years ago one of our readers wrote us that soaking whites in a strong solution of hot water and a dishwasher detergent such as Cascade or Calgonite will make whites come out sparkling. (After soaking, wash as usual.) We've tried it; it really works! Caution: don't do this each time you wash, as the detergent contains lye and eventually, with overuse, could harm your clothes.

Fels-Naptha

A.B. of Stowe, Vermont, wrote us to say: "This is to sing the praises of an old-fashioned bar of golden Fels-Naptha soap. So many uses, including for fine silk washables—worth turning to these days when having a small silk scarf dry-cleaned costs as much as the scarf itself (if bought a score of years ago, when money grew on trees). Anyway, this soap is a good friend." To iron those silks that we washed, we gently press out the water, put them in a plastic bag, and stick them in the freezer. When it finally becomes crisis time and we *have* to attack the monstrous ironing piles, our silks are damp, fresh, and ready to be ironed.

TAR

⊠⊠⊠

Q What can I use on a woolen blanket to remove tar from a hot afternoon on the roof?

J.M.
Montpelier, Vermont

A To remove the tar from your blanket, all you need is "Goop," available in the laundry section of most supermarkets. Rub into the tar spots on your blanket, scrape off the excess, and then wash in cool water. Hang to dry. Incidentally, our market was recently out of this wonder product, and as it was originally sold as a waterless hand cleaner we went looking for it at our local automotive supply store. We asked for Goop and were handed a large tube of adhesive! So readers, beware: there are two products named Goop and the adhesive is NOT the product we recommend for use in your laundry. We finally did purchase another brand-name waterless cleaner, but it proved to be much less effective than Goop, at least as far as spots, stains, grease, and grime on our clothes was concerned.

MILDEW

⊠⊠⊠

Q I have draperies with acrylic foam backing, 58 percent cotton and 42 percent polyester, machine washable; color: arctic white. The lower half of the drapes have a mass of mildew on them. What can I do to get the mildew out before I machine wash them?

M.S.
Springfield, Vermont

A We've had great luck with a mixture of one part Lysol to one part water. Saturate the mildewed portion of the curtain and let sit for about ½ hour, then go over the surface lightly with a brush. Put the curtains (unrinsed) in the washer and wash as usual. Caution: spot test a small area of the material first. We've also heard that soaking fabrics in sour milk will remove mildew, but we've never tried it—we seem unable to keep milk around long enough for it to *turn* sour . . . or, according to our long-suffering families, never seem to have any milk around at all.

NAIL POLISH

Q My daughter got fingernail polish on her white Ben & Jerry's Ice Cream sweatshirt. I have tried to remove it with fingernail polish remover, which did nothing. Do you have any suggestions?

A.M.
Montpelier, Vermont

A An acetate-based nail polish remover, plain acetone (available at paint and hardware stores), or denatured alcohol will do the trick if applied while the nail polish is still wet. Once it has hardened, it's a bear to remove from fabric. The only things left to try if the sweatshirt is an all-natural fiber (and we hope that the manufacturers of all-natural ice cream would promote their product with all-natural-fiber sweatshirts) are Goop and/or bleach. Rub Goop into the stain, let sit awhile, then handwash in bleach and water. Incidentally, we first heard of Goop's many uses from a woman who signed herself "Grammy," Fair Haven. She told us it worked wonders on grass stains, and we subsequently found it works wonders on just about any other stain and blotch. It is also much more economical than other prewash laundry products. It has taken a place of honor among our other favorite multipurpose household/laundry aids: vinegar, dish detergent, baking soda, and denture cleanser!

Color Fastness

To keep the dye in new clothes from running, soak first in 3 cups water, 1 cup vinegar, and ¼ cup salt for a couple of hours, then wash as usual.

STIFF DENIM

Q I recently made myself a denim jumper. Despite repeated washings, the denim continues to be as stiff as cardboard. Any suggestions as to how to get the fabric soft and comfortable?

MRS. H.
White River Junction, Vermont

A Buy some fabric softener, fill a bucket with warm water, and put in about ½ cup of softener. Mix well and pop your jumper into the mixture. Let it sit for several hours, then launder. We've done this with new blue jeans and it works like a charm!

LINEN

▧▧

Q Where will I get my *large* white linen tablecloth, which belonged to my grandmother, washed and ironed? Our local cleaners say they will wash it, but won't iron it! If you are unable to answer this before the holidays are over, I'll just hopefully hang on to the soiled tablecloth!

S.F.
Montpelier, Vermont

A The bad news is that by the time this gets printed in the paper, the holidays will be over. The good news is that we managed to find a laundry near you that will wash and iron your tablecloth. But, be forewarned: because your tablecloth is linen and old, the proprietor of the laundry asked us to tell you that he reserves the right to turn the job down. "If linen hasn't been taken care of properly," he said, "it can become quite fragile, and although we use a gentle cycle in the machine, our laundry soap is stronger than the home product . . . we want to be sure we won't harm her tablecloth." Also, though we don't want to sound gloomy, if your tablecloth has been soiled for some time, there is a good chance that it won't come completely clean. It's a good idea to remove food stains as soon as possible. On finer fabrics, such as linen, a good rub over the spot with Ivory soap or Fels-Naptha (bar type) followed by a flush with hot water will usually do the trick. For spilled wine, sprinkle immediately with table salt, and for fruit stains or fruit juice spills, treat at once with lemon juice and rinse with cold water.

Q We have a family tradition and two years ago, on my wedding day, my mother-in-law gave me a white linen tablecloth. Each guest was asked to sign the tablecloth in pencil. I was to stitch over each name with embroidery floss. My problem is that one guest signed in ink. I was very sad to see this as I am afraid the ink will run and spoil the tablecloth when I wash it. Can either of you suggest how I can deal with this? The tablecloth is meant to be a keepsake of my special day.

CLAIRE
Hydeville, Vermont

A First, attack the offending signature with rubbing alcohol, then wash with dishwasher liquid. Although the ink may not come out completely, it will be removed enough so that you needn't worry about it running when you launder your tablecloth . . . and in fact the image may be readable enough so you can embroider over the name (should you still want to!). We have been told that there are ink removers sold in stationery stores, but have never been able to find them up in this neck of the woods.

QUILT CARE

Q I have an old quilt that has what looks like rust spots on it and also what I can only describe as age stains. Is there any safe way to get these out?

G.A.
Middlebury, Vermont

A You may find this hard to believe, but we came across this in one of our quilting magazines. Procter & Gamble puts out a sheep shampoo called Orvus: it comes in a paste, is very mild, and will take out the kind of spots and stains you describe without in any way harming the quilt. You can find it at feed and grain stores or at places that carry farm supplies. It's also great for washing fine woolens and your hair. While we're on the subject of using animal care products for human needs . . . Bag Balm, used for treating sore and chapped udders, is wonderful for use on everything from chapped and wind burned skin to squeaky bedsprings. A horse-grooming product called Mane and Tail is a terrific hair conditioner, and a lady of our acquaintance uses Hoof Maker to strengthen her fingernails.

FABRIC CARE AND PRESERVATION

BABY CLOTHES

▽▽

Q Please tell me what to do for baby clothes of sixty years ago. They are of satin and wool cashmere and sure have yellowed.

C.J.B.
Barre, Vermont

A We're afraid there isn't much that can be done, as the yellowing is due to the normal oxidation of fibers. Like rusting with iron, this oxidation is a chemical reaction of the fibers with oxygen in the air. This can be prevented by storing the clothes properly in the first place. We recommend the use of "acid-free" tissue paper, which is used by museums. You can order it through a catalogue issued by University Products, Inc., P.O. Box 101, Holyoke, MA 01401. The catalogue, incidentally, offers a full range of conservation supplies for museums, libraries, and just plain folk. An item they stock which may be of particular interest to our readers who wish to preserve family papers or memorabilia is their Heritage Album, which contains, among other things, photo pages, binders for personal papers, and see-through display sheets, all of which are acid-free.

DEAR ANNE AND NAN -

WEDDING DRESS

Q In looking through an old trunk, I came upon a lovely satin flapper-style wedding dress encrusted with tiny seed pearls and lace, dating back to 1926. I want to have it cleaned but our local dry-cleaning establishments will not attempt it. I am looking for a cleaners that will clean it. Can you help?

L.B.
Barre, Vermont

A To better answer your question, we phoned Meredith Wright of Montpelier, Vermont, an expert on fabric restoration and conservation. Meredith explained that normally, dry cleaners use a solvent chemical in their machines to dissolve dirt; also these machines tumble the garments (think of the solvent as a soap in a regular washing machine). Meredith said if the dress were hers, she would sit down at the phone and try to find a dry cleaner who would agree to use fresh solvent and not tumble the dress. Using the washing machine analogy again, she said it would be like soaking an item or using the delicate cycle. She said there are cleaners in cities (though not around here) who specialize in hand cleaning garments. She also noted that many stains in old garments just won't come out, no matter what. "If there are tan-colored stains, for instance," she noted, "it's probably from sugar that was in punch or champagne, and when sugar oxidizes, it caramelizes." Go to your public library and borrow a phone book of a city near you (in your case, Boston or New York). Look under "Dry Cleaning" and you'll find that some of the display ads will note that the establishment does "specialty cleaning." Then give them a ring.

REVITALIZING VELVET

▽▽

Q How do you restore an even nap to a velvet dress that became crushed in my overcrowded closet?

C.B.
Walpole, New Hampshire

A If the velvet is "bruised," place the area, pile side down, over the bristles of a brush. Hold a steam iron just above the fabric, letting the steam pour through the pile. Shake out fabric until partially dry, then let it dry the rest of the way by itself. If the entire dress is bruised or crushed, lay a damp (almost wet) towel on the wrong side of the fabric, and with an iron set on its high setting, iron. Turn the dress right side out and brush up the nap with a soft brush.

WOOLENS

Q Would you please advise on the best way to protect woolens that are folded in a drawer from moths and other insects besides using mothballs? I have seen fresheners, etc., to hang in closets but have not come across anything for drawers.

D.E.
Chittenden, Vermont

Again, an answer from Meredith Wright. Her response is as follows:

Eternal vigilance is the price of liberty from moth damage. The creature that does the damage is the larval stage of the clothing moth, so if you see little ½-inch moths fluttering around, it's too late. They will munch wool and, to a lesser extent, silk. This is in preference to cotton or linen, as wool and silk are made of protein. They will munch feathers and fur even in preference to wool or silk, and will head for any food stains in preference to clean clothes.

What can be done? The answer will be somewhat different for modern clothes than for heirlooms, as modern clothes can better withstand the tumbling action of dry-cleaning machines.

MODERN CLOTHES

1. Thoroughly vacuum the inside of the drawer before putting anything away. Moth eggs are tiny and develop quickly into voracious larvae. The best way to keep an eye on what's in there is to paint the inside of the drawer, preferably white. Drawer paper is not a good idea, because the creatures can hide from view underneath it. A piece of white cloth or an old sheet is a good alternative as it can be taken out and easily laundered.
2. Make sure the clothes are clean before they are put away. Dry cleaning is a good idea just before storage, even if you otherwise handwash your woolens and silks . . . the dry-cleaning chemicals kill the insects.
3. Mothballs and moth flakes are useless as far as killing moth eggs, and they'll only work for the other stages in an airtight container, which most drawers usually aren't. If you must use them, put them in a cloth bag so that they are not in direct contact with the clothes. Do not use them in plastic bags, as their vapors may cause the plastic to "melt" on your clothes.

4. Eternal vigilance: every couple of weeks, *look in the drawer*. If you see any moths, larvae, castings, or dust, remove the clothes, shake them out, and clean the drawer thoroughly.

HEIRLOOMS

Most of what has been said above still applies, but usually it is not a good idea to send heirloom clothing to the dry cleaners. A light brushing outdoors in the light (moths and larvae hate light) and vacuuming the drawers periodically will go a long way to help. Keep things with good hiding places—such as muffs, feather pillows, comforters and quilts with wool batting, mittens, and fur pieces—away from other garments.

If something is really infested but has great sentimental value, it may be worth sending to the dry cleaners despite the risk of damage: the piece will be lost anyway without treatment. Talk to the dry cleaners about whether there is a "gentle" cycle or other careful treatment that could be used.

Old-fashioned Moth Protection
Scatter dried bay leaves in the drawers and between layers of the clothing you wish to store. Moths will stay away!

DOG AND CAT HAIR

Q Do you know of any way that one can get dog and cat hair off a black cashmere coat? I visited a friend's house recently who also happens to be an animal lover and when I put my coat on to leave, it was just covered! A clothes brush gets some, but not all of it, off. Any suggestions?

R.M.
Cavendish, Vermont

A Anne and Nan (and their visitors) have been dealing with this problem for years, and Anne has found (revolting as this may sound) that nothing works better than spit applied to the fingers . . . then "finger-brush" the hairs off. However, this method may not, understandably, be everyone's cup of tea. Here are some other suggestions.

Wrap wide adhesive tape, sticky side out, around your hand. The animal hair will stick to the tape. Or wrap (again, wrong side out) a rolled-up piece of newspaper with masking tape and roll it over the garment. Final suggestion: place the garment (dry) in your clothes dryer with a damp towel and tumble dry for about 15 minutes. All the above will remove lint as well.

CLEANING LEATHER AND SUEDE

SLUSH AND SALT

Q With winter around the corner, I would like to know how to remove slush and salt stains from shoes or boots—leather, suede, or nylon trim. Many thanks.

E.R.B.
Burlington, Vermont

A The old tried-and-true method for removing salt and slush stains is to mix one part warm water to one part vinegar. Sponge off. Try to get the salt/slush off your footwear as soon as possible: the longer it stays on, the stubborner it is to remove.

For leather, try to give your boots a good rubdown with saddle soap at least once a month during the winter (available at most leather-goods stores and all tack shops): follow the directions on the can. If your leather boots are good ones, follow up with an application of Lexol (a leather conditioner) or mink oil, which both conditions and waterproofs. Finally, give your boots a good polish with any commercial shoe polish.

For suede, follow up the application of the vinegar/water with a suede brush, then spray on Suede Saver, which is a silicone water repellent.

SOFT LEATHER

Q I have my son's soft leather jacket that, when it comes back from the cleaners, isn't clean. Is there a home remedy for cleaning, i.e., special soap or whatever?

A.S.
Rutland, Vermont

A If there are some stubborn spots, try using rubbing alcohol. Brush lightly with a stiff brush. If you want to attempt washing the jacket yourself, C. W. of Burlington, Vermont, sent us in the following "recipe": "To wash, use real soap (Ivory or Fels-Naptha), not a detergent. (I save leftover bits of hand and bath soap.) Make a fairly rich lather, repeatedly rubbing in and scraping off the leather until lather comes clean. Then use a somewhat lighter lather to rinse. Do not rinse in plain water. Roll up in a Turkish towel and dry away from the heat. I usually replace the towel daily. If the leather is too stiff after it dries, the rinsing lather was too thin. Correct by rewetting in heavier soapsuds. Linings should be removed— they might get sticky."

SUEDE

Q Any suggestions as to how to clean some dirt spots off a suede jacket?

A.C.
Cavendish, Vermont

A Wish you had told us what kind of dirt. If it's just dirt dirt (i.e., a mud splash or the like), you can probably clean the spots with a suede brush. Otherwise, please send your jacket to a dry cleaner. For suede clothing of any kind, the best way to care for it is prevention. When you buy the garment, spray it with Suede Saver or Scotchgard, both of which repel dirt.

LEATHER CARE

Q Do you know how I can prevent my leather products from cracking?

P.B.
Barre, Vermont

A To maintain leather, we use saddle soap. This helps keep the leather supple.

R.K. of Mendon, Vermont, sent us the following "recipe": "For dry leather, first liberally brush on the following formula . . . I know it sounds strange but it is straight from old-time southern horsemen, and I know it works. I've used it exclusively for nearly fifteen years and all my tack and leather goods are in wonderful condition. Mix 3 quarts of kerosene, 3 cups pure neat's-foot oil (NOT neat's-foot *compound*), and 1 cup peanut oil. Shake it up, brush it on, and then clean with saddle soap. Use only the glycerin bar soap—not the yellow stuff that comes in cans."

**READER
FEEDBACK**

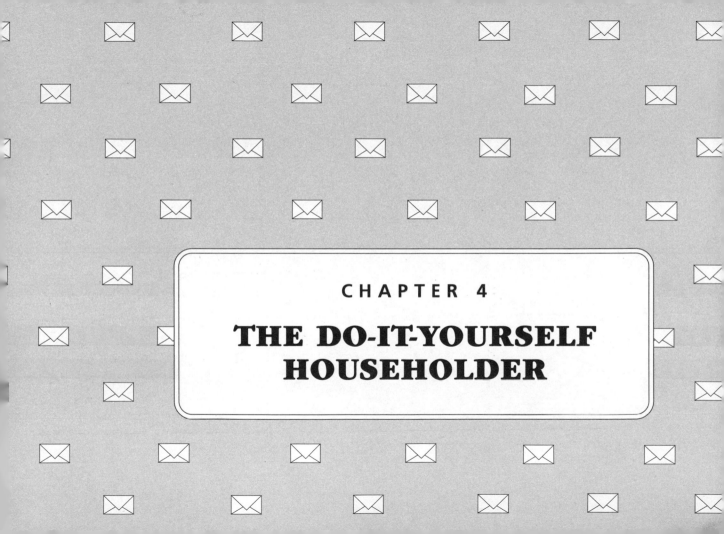

CHAPTER 4

THE DO-IT-YOURSELF HOUSEHOLDER

Over the years, we have discovered that the most important thing to remember when one is going to "do it yourself" is to have all the tools, materials, etc., you are going to need assembled before you start the job. This is a help in that it not only requires you to review the steps of work that the job entails, but will save the inevitable frustration that occurs when, halfway through the job, you discover that you have mislaid, seemingly forever, your only Phillips screwdriver or that the staples you or your housemate used up a couple of months or years ago have never been replaced.

REPAIRS AND RESTORATION

WOOD PANELING

Q Could you give me directions on how to paint wood paneling? I would like to paint my living room paneling white.

V.A.
Worcester, Vermont

A If your paneling is varnished, gently roughen the surface with fine steel wool, then prime and paint. Be sure to use an oil-base paint, as latex will not adhere to a varnished surface. If the paneling is not varnished but has been waxed and/ or polished over the years, first clean the surface with a detergent-and-water solution. Then take a cloth saturated with paint thinner and rub with the grain until the cloth comes clean. Let dry thoroughly, prime, and paint.

Q My husband and I recently bought an old house and the kitchen has varnished wood cabinet doors that look, to put it kindly, somewhat the worse for wear. We'd like to redo them so that the wood (which we think is nice wood) will show in its natural state. Any suggestions?

E.W.A.
Windsor, Vermont

Paintbrushes

If you hate cleaning both oil- and latex-filled paintbrushes at the end of every day's work as much as we do, just wrap the dirty brush in cling wrap and stick it in the freezer. When you are ready to start your paint job again, unwrap the brush and run under hot water for a few seconds . . . and you're ready to go!

C.M. of Manchester, Vermont, wrote us with the following invaluable hint. "Here's a tip for painters, professional or otherwise: The paint solvent bin seems to dry out paintbrushes before you finish painting. Often, I would end up tossing paintbrushes out. Now they get a second chance when I clean them in a solution of Cascade (dishwasher detergent) and water. They come out looking brand new. My painter laughed until he tried it. . . . No more laughing!"

A First, we think you'll find the job a lot easier if you remove your cabinet doors. With paint remover (such as Zip-Strip) remove the varnish. Then, depending on what you uncover, you can do the following: (1) Coat with two coats of Minwax. This comes in a variety of wood shades and will preserve and protect your wood. Polish with a hard paste wax. (2) If you prefer that your wood look shiny, paint with any polyurethane-base varnish. This will make your cupboards easier to clean, incidentally. (3) If you don't like the color of your wood once it is all cleaned off and wish to give it a shiny finish, first apply a wood sealant (these also come in a variety of shades) and then, when thoroughly dry, paint with polyurethane.

WOOD FURNITURE

Q How do you get water marks off wood furniture?

L.L.
Woodstock, Vermont

A Wish you'd told us whether the marks are black or white . . . anyway, we'll give you the solution for both. For white marks, use a combination of salt and mineral oil. Have a dish of table salt and one of mineral oil. Dip finger in oil, then in salt, and rub. When the spot has gone, wipe with soft dry cloth and polish. You can also use cigar or cigarette ash and boiled linseed oil. Following the grain of the wood, wipe ash lightly into the spot, then wipe area with a cloth dipped in linseed oil.

For black marks caused by water (use this procedure only on wood that has an oil finish or a penetrating-sealer finish): Scrub spot with 4/0 steel wool saturated with a denatured alcohol solvent. Rub hard in the direction of the grain. When the black stain has gone, renew old finish with a cleanser/conditioner (1 part gum turpentine to 3 parts boiled linseed oil floated on the surface of a small container of hot water: with clean dry cloth, skim along warm, oily layer floating on the surface and wipe wood in the direction of the grain).

To prevent your furniture from being marked by condensation from flower vases, glue a rubber canning jar ring to the bottom of the vase.

Q I have acquired a mahogany dining table and buffet that have been in my husband's family. I tried to polish the table with "Old English" lemon oil and it streaks and does not give a shine. Can you tell me how to clean it and what I should be using for polish?

M.A.
Waterbury, Vermont

A The reason you get streaking is that years of wax, dust, and general grime have accumulated on the surface of the wood. Your first step is to clean your buffet and dining table with warm water and either Murphy Oil Soap or Joy: do *not* use a detergent. Then, take paint thinner (*not* stripper) and a clean, lint-free cloth and rub lightly with the grain of the wood; finish up with another clean cloth until cloth and wood are free of old wax and dirt. Finally, apply a coat of Minwax Finishing Wax (use the kind made for dark surfaces). If the surface appears streaky, apply a second coat. Polish with a soft cloth. If you wish to polish the furniture on an ongoing basis, we have gotten glowing recommendations for two products: one is Scott's Liquid Gold, which is available in many supermarkets across the country. The other is Sani-Wax. You can send for a free sample to Joann Champion, New Horizons, P.O. Box 769, Andover Road, Chester, VT 05143. Both these products will remove dirt and grime and prevent waxy buildup.

MARBLE

Q Can you tell me how to clean an all-white marble monument that is stained by birds and the weather? Can it be waxed for protection and with what, providing you can find something to clean it with in the first place?

E.M.K.
Springfield, Vermont

A You can clean the monument with full-strength Clorox and a scrub brush, then rinse down well with water. Unless the stone is highly polished, wax is not recommended for use on gravestones or monuments by most people who deal with marble. However, if you decide you do want to wax the monument, use a white or carnauba-type wax. A better product to use as a sealer is something called Bond-Dri, which is available at many large hardware supply stores. If you can't find it on the shelves, look in your yellow pages under "Monuments" and call around to a few monument dealers: you'll probably find it's available from at least one of them. As marble is so extremely porous, even Bond-Dri is not guaranteed to seal it against future staining.

We were advised by a number of readers that the best way to clean your monument is professionally: most monument dealers have a cleaning service. Gerald Racetts, manager at Gawett Marble and Granite, Center Rutland, VT 05736, told us that our advice to E.M.K. might—depending on factors such as density, water absorption, abrasive hardness, etc.—turn the marble a yellowish color. "Each problem with marble is a unique one in itself," he wrote, "and should be dealt with accordingly." He included a brochure on "The Care and Cleaning of Marble," which he said is available, at no cost, from Gawett. He requests that you enclose a self-addressed, double-stamped envelope.

READER FEEDBACK

Q We have several pieces of marble which go on bureaus we are refinishing. The marble is chipped, yellowed, and stained. How do we go about getting the marble to look good again? Is there a sealer we should put on top to keep it nice and preserve it? Also, if we cannot do the marble tops ourselves, is there somewhere we can take them to to be redone?

S.R.
Mount Holly, Vermont

A You can do it yourself, although it's a somewhat arduous process. If you would prefer having someone do it for you, most monument companies, having both the necessary equipment and expertise, will clean not only gravestones but "household" marble as well. However, if you decide to do it yourself, here's how.

To remove stains, assuming they are from something organic such as tea, juice, flowers, etc., you need 20 percent strength hydrogen peroxide and powdered whiting, which is sold in most paint and hardware stores. Mix a poultice of whiting and hydrogen peroxide to form a thick paste. Apply a ½-inch layer of this mixture over the stain. To keep the poultice from drying out too quickly, cover it with a piece of plastic cling wrap and hold it in place with masking tape. Leave on overnight, and if the stain is really stubborn, leave on for 48 hours.

After cleaning, if you wish to hand polish the marble, you'll need (1) wet/dry sandpaper (silicon carbide) in grits of 80, 120, 220, 400, and 600 (available at auto supply stores), (2) tin oxide or pumice powder (available at hardware stores), (3) a clean white rag, and (4) water. Starting with the lowest grit number, dip the sandpaper in water (this keeps it from getting clogged with marble dust), sand, and let dry. Proceed with the next-higher grade of paper and repeat this process until the 600 grade is achieved. Dampen the cloth and apply a small amount of the polishing powder (tin oxide or pumice powder). Rub the stone until a change in the surface can be detected: flush the stone with water and let dry. Buff with a dry cloth. You can seal the marble with a hard, carnauba-type wax or sealer.

Q A 1-inch-thick marble top to a chest needs repair. It has a white beveled edge and lost a corner in a fall, about 3 inches by 4 inches. Not lost, really, but broken off and available. Kindly suggest a mending procedure for the homeowner or, if this is not practical, how about a repair service, please?

A.B.
Ascutney, Vermont

A You can mend your chest top with an epoxy-type glue . . . even Krazy Glue will do the job. Just be sure that both sides of the pieces you are going to glue are clean and dust-free.

PHONOGRAPH RECORDS

Q I would like some information on the least damaging way to clean phonograph records which include some early ones as well as more recent ones. These are not just dusty records; some have actually been well-coated with particles of drywall and dust which attached so firmly that they do not come off with a dry rag. Also, are there any record dealers in this state or the New England area?

J.L.
Rutland, Vermont

A Put away your rag, J.L.! Holding the record vertically, use a hair dryer set on High to blow off the drywall and dust. Then, with a very fine artist's paintbrush, brush the record, going with the grooves. Finally, use a Discwasher (brand name—available at record stores) to finish the job. This is a very fine brush with one-directional bristles and the equivalent of a lint brush for records.

There are many record dealers in New England, and nationwide as well. Many of them are listed, according to specialty, in a book called *American Premium Record Guide*, third edition, 1915–1965, by R. L. Docks, published by Books Americana and distributed by Charles Tuttle Company, Rutland, Vermont. This volume is full of information, including a section entitled "Where to Buy, Trade or Sell Records." It's published in paperback and costs $14.95.

SLIPPERY TOBOGGAN BOTTOM

Q We have an old wooden toboggan that we'd like to have ready for the sliding season. Currently, the wood is bare on the bottom. What would be a protective, long-lasting coating to put on the bottom that wouldn't slow the slide?

J.F.W.
Brandon, Vermont

A Make sure any old finish has been completely removed, then seal the wood with at least three coats of marine varnish or marine polyurethane. When this has dried thoroughly, polish the surface with a hard wax such as carnauba or Minwax polish. Happy sliding!

DEAR ANNE AND NAN -

STERLING SILVER JEWELRY

Q What is the best way to clean and care for sterling silver jewelry?

TARNISHED
Wilder, Vermont

A Make up a solution of ½ cup clear ammonia, ½ cup warm water, and 1 tablespoon of a mild liquid detergent. Depending on how tarnished the silver is, soak it in the solution for up to an hour. Rinse under warm tap water until there is no remaining trace of ammonia. Put the jewelry on a clean towel and dry thoroughly . . . or dry with a hair dryer set on High.

As the reaction of silver to oxygen (i.e., air) causes tarnishing, store your silver in a cloth pouch or wrap it in tissue paper.

To Clean Unlacquered Brass Jewelry

Dilute a packet of orange Kool-Aid according to instructions on the pack; soak jewelry in mixture until tarnish is gone. Then wash with warm, soapy water. Dry thoroughly.

ARTS AND CRAFTS

HOT-IRON TRANSFER

Q Thirty-five years ago I used a hot-iron transfer, but kept the paper it was on. For one reason or another, I don't have the picture I embroidered and would like to do another one. Is there anyone who can take this very fragile paper and do a transfer? I have tried using a purple transfer pen but the paper is too prone to tear. It is a very simple picture, 14" × 18", and just an outline stitch of a collie on a hill.

MRS. D.K.
North Clarendon, Vermont

A Thanks to the miracles of modern technology, we think your problem may be solved. Take your transfer to the nearest photocopy machine (your bank or local library is your best bet) and photocopy the pattern. Hold the transferred pattern against a window or some other light source and trace on the *wrong* side with your transfer pen. Then iron on to your fabric as usual and you'll have a pattern exactly like, and just as clear as, the original.

Recipe for Sugar Starch to Shape Crochet

Put together one part water to one part sugar: bring to a full boil to dissolve sugar, cool, and use full-strength.

KNITTED DISHCLOTHS/WASHCLOTHS

Q I was wondering if you could tell me where I could get a pattern for knitted dishcloths? I have heard everybody talking about how nice and easy they are, but I haven't been able to find a pattern.

P.F.
Barre, Vermont

A Mrs. M.W. of Cavendish, Vermont, sent us this one. Materials: 1 ball J. P. Coates Knit Cro-Sheen Art A-64 No. 1 White and a few yards of No. 13 Shaded Blue, No. 5 knitting needles, 1 steel crochet hook No. 1/0. Gauge: 5 stitches with doubled thread = 1 inch.

Using double thread, cast on 51 stitches. Work in garter stitch for 1 inch. Next row (eyelet row): k 2, *k 2 together, yarn over, k 2.* Repeat from * across to last stitch; knit last stitch. Continue in garter stitch until total length is 9 inches. Next row: knit eyelet row as before. Continue in garter stitch for 1 inch more. Bind off in knitting. Border: with 2 strands Shaded Blue together, crochet straight chain stitches evenly around edge, making 3 straight chain stitches in each corner.

WOODWORKING PATTERNS

Q I am looking for woodworking patterns for lawn ornaments and the big butterflies you see made from plywood. Also, do you know where I can find a pattern for an Adirondack chair?

MARTIN
Waterbury, Vermont

A Write to Craft Patterns Studio, 3N345 North 12th Street, St. Charles, IL 60174, for their catalogue of lawn ornament patterns. If your local lumberyard doesn't carry Easi-Bild patterns (they have patterns for lawn ornaments, bird houses, furniture—including Adirondack chairs—etc.), write the firm at Easi-Bild Pattern Company, Box 2383-15241, Pleasantville, NY 10570.

Other good sources of patterns and plans are *Popular Mechanics*, *Workbench*, and *Grit Paper* magazines.

BRAIDED RUG SUPPLIES

Q Can you tell me where I can buy wool material for use in braided rugs and heavy cord for lacing them?

H.S.
Pawlet, Vermont

A A company called Braid-Aid, 466 Washington Street, Pembroke, MA 02359, has, reputedly, the largest inventory of materials and supplies for braiding, hooking, spinning, and quilting in the country. They sell wool remnants by the pound at a very reasonable price. For specially dyed wools their price is somewhat higher. They will be happy to send you their catalogue for $4. Other good sources for wool material are yard sales, tag sales, recycling centers, and secondhand shops.

PERIOD CLOTHING PATTERNS

Q   I am looking for sewing patterns for period clothing. In particular, the 1920s era. Could you tell me where I can write to find these patterns?

PATTY
Rutland, Vermont

A   We've come up with a few sources for you. K.K. of Wallingford, Vermont, wrote: "Folkwear patterns that feature ethnic, frontier, and 'timeless' clothing from 1850 to 1950 were unavailable for a while, but due to public outcry are being reprinted by Taunton Press, 63 South Main Street, P.O. Box 5506, Newton, CT 06470-5506. They also publish an excellent crafts magazine for serious fiber artists and hobbyists called *Threads*."

Our old friend and advisor, Meredith Wright of Montpelier, let us know about a company that carries historic patterns: Amazon Drygoods, 2218 East 11th Street, Davenport, IA 52803-3760. For $5 you can send for a catalogue of authentic historical patterns to Past Patterns, P.O. Box 7587, Grand Rapids, MI 49510. And finally, Meredith herself has recently published a book called *Put on Thy Beautiful Garments: Rural New England Clothing, 1783–1800*. The book contains a great wealth of historical information as well as pattern diagrams and instructions. To order, write to The Clothes Press, P.O. Box 686, Montpelier, VT 05601-0686. Enclose check or money order for $12.50 plus $3.00 for shipping and handling.

THREAD SOURCES

Q Due to the continually increasing cost of thread, I am wondering if you know how and where thread can be purchased wholesale. The cost of thread, especially the "dual-duty cotton polyester" (which appears to be the most durable quality) has increased 20 cents in the past two months. Also, many times the last quarter of a spool of thread will be poorly wound and twisted. When one sews for the public and does alterations, not all clients can purchase their own thread, which is now almost $2 a spool, or to have the added cost passed on to them. Suggestion and addresses of thread companies would be helpful!

P.M.
Brandon, Vermont

A M.D. of Plainfield, Vermont, came up with two sources, and says they both have catalogues: Home-Sew, Bethlehem, PA 18018, and Newark Dressmakers Supply, 6473 Ruch Road, P.O. Box 20730, Lehigh Valley, PA 18002-0730. She writes: "Both of these places have thread on a 600-yard spool, all different kinds and colors. I do all kinds of sewing and crafts and can't find the things I need around here. Dressmakers Supply has just about everything one would ever need."

ZIPPER TAPES

Q Over the years, I've been removing zippers from the old clothes that I use for making rags for rag rugs. Does anyone have any ideas of what I can do with them?

A.S.
Rutland, Vermont

A E.B. wrote us to say, "My father worked for a company that made zippers before his retirement in 1967. He brought home some odd rolls of the tape—double coils (about 6 inches in diameter) which contained quite a few yards. I'm still using the last of them for a variety of purposes; unzipped I use them for tying packages and as plant ties, for instance. Even a 7-inch piece allows a twist around the plant stake before knotting at the stake to keep from chafing the plant."

MAGIC ROCKS

Q My husband would like to know how to make magic rocks with bluing. I have heard of them being made from coal, ammonia, and bluing. Can you help?

S.C.
Barre, Vermont

A The "magic rocks" also used to be called Depression gardens or crystal gardens. We have not one but two recipes! The first: place three or four pieces of any kind of coal or coke in an open glass dish. If using charcoal, add a few extra pieces. Pour 2 tablespoons each of water, liquid bluing, and common table salt over the coal. Let stand 24 hours. Then add 2 tablespoons more of salt. On the third day, add 2 tablespoons of clear ammonia to give a fluffy appearance. The chemical reactions will create a beautiful bowl of flowers or coral, depending how you look at it.

The second recipe: Place broken pieces of terra cotta in a glass bowl or jar. Pour the following solution over them: 4 teaspoons water, 1 teaspoon ammonia, 4 teaspoons bluing, 1 teaspoon Mercurochrome, 4 teaspoons salt. Add more of this solution each day until the magic rocks, crystal garden, or Depression garden has grown to desired size.

Potato Glue

We received this hint in a letter from M. L., age eighty-eight, of Springfield, Vermont. "Over the years," she wrote, "the best glue I can find is a cold boiled potato. Break, don't cut, in two and rub on paper as you would any glue. Press with hand for a minute or less. It has held my snapshots since 1910, as well as cut-out recipes. I had my pupils use it in school with good results and it's less messy than any paste."

RECYCLED SOAP

Q We would like to know if there is a way to process or melt soap chips into liquid soap. We've tried melting but it hardens even if water is added. Do you know of any ingredients we could add to keep it liquid?

M.S. and J.A.
East Montpelier, Vermont

A Just put your soap chips in a blender with a little water . . . instant liquid soap! If you wish, you can also melt the soap with water over low heat and then add a few drops of glycerin (available at your local drugstore). Store in a closed container. If you want to make recycled soap from soap ends, K.M. of Pittsford, Vermont, sent us the following recipe: "(1) With an electric blender, powder soap ends as fine as possible. (2) Place 1 cup of powder into a bowl and add several drops of food coloring, 1 tablespoon perfume (optional), and 3 table-

A Final Soap Hint

D.C. wrote us: "I put small pieces of soap into a small mesh bag and tie the top. This can be used for washing hands. The mesh acts as a scrub brush while the soap cleans. One can add small pieces of soap when they are available."

spoons water. (3) Mix ingredients with fork until the consistency of pie dough, then knead into a soft clay. If necessary, add a little more water. (4) Using fingers, mold the soap into balls 2 inches in diameter. (5) Lay finished soaps on waxed paper to dry for several days. When completely dry, rub with a nylon stocking for a satin-smooth finish. Makes 8–9 balls."

EARTHENWARE CROCK

Q My problem: a large earthenware crock which has, I discovered last fall to my sorrow, a "hairline" crack . . . in short, it leaks. Do you have any remedy for sealing the base of the crack?

J.E.
Calais, Vermont

A If you don't put anything hot into your crock, we've found paraffin or candle wax to be a great sealer. We've used both on our earthenware crocks and over pinhole leaks in pieces of antique tinware we use for flower vases. If you know where the crack is, you can also seal it with Borden's Elmer's Glue. We don't recommend you use any of the "super glues" if you have ever used your crock for pickle making, as the salt from the brine permeates the earthenware—the "super glue" just won't stick.

SOAP SCUM

Q What can one use in drains to keep them from plugging due to using too much soap?

M.A.
Rutland, Vermont

A According to an old book of household hints in our possession, "Waste pipes may be cleaned of soap and slime by putting a handful of common salt down the drain overnight." S.B. wrote us with the following suggestion: "Pour a cup of cider vinegar into the drain and follow with a teakettleful of boiling water. It has always worked. Do this once a week to keep the scum down."

SPILLED URETHANE

Q How can I remove urethane from no-wax linoleum that the builder spilled in several areas in every room and even on the hot-air register? We've tried everything and nothing so far works.

MRS. R.D.
Waterbury, Vermont

A To clean up the spilled urethane, use a clean white rag dampened with either charcoal lighter fluid or turpentine. Rinse the area with plain water. It is *very* important that the cleaned area not be walked on for at least 30 minutes.

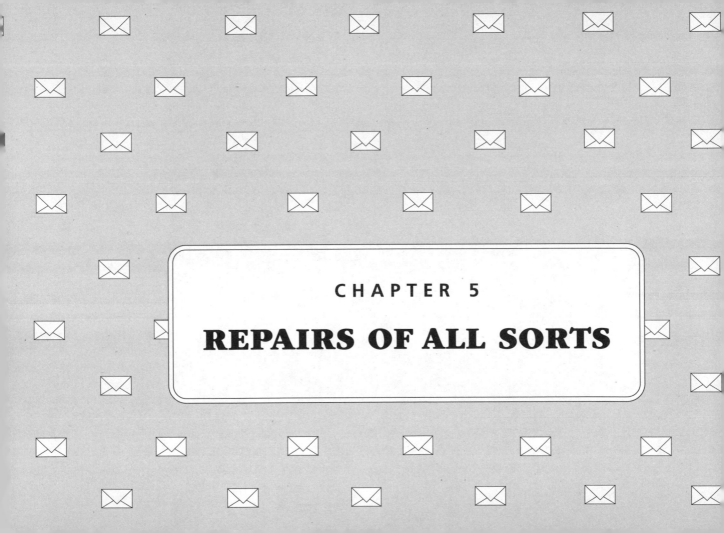

CHAPTER 5

REPAIRS OF ALL SORTS

Yankees are known for their thrift. We hate to throw things out and are tenacious in our pursuit of repair persons. We find people to reweave moth holes, grind chipped crystal, and re-tin church-dinner baking sheets. All communities should be blessed as we are with people like Mort Stillings ("the Factotum") of Montpelier, who can repair just about anything.

BAROMETER

Q My grandmother left me an old wall barometer which needs to be repaired. I've taken it to several jewelers and no one could fix it. Any ideas?

SALLY
Shrewsbury, Vermont

A There's a gent who advertises in the *National Association of Watch and Clock Collectors* magazine who makes and repairs barometers as well as buys antique models. His name is Neville Lewis, his address is HCR 68, Box 130L, Cushing, ME 04563, and his phone is 207-354-8055.

BRISTLE REPLACEMENT

Q A man at an antique shop in Quechee, Vermont, suggested that I write to you. Is there anyone who will insert new bristles into a beautiful antique hairbrush?

P.S.
Punxsutawney, Pennsylvania

A Thanks to one of our faithful readers, B.W. of Perkinsville, we can answer your query. The Orum Silver Company at P.O. Box 805, 51 South Vine Street, Meriden, CT 06450, replaces bristles. This custom work is expensive. Nylon bristles cost $110 and boar bristles cost $125.

BOOK BINDING

Q I recently bought two old leather-bound books at a yard sale. The bindings are falling apart and I'd like to get them repaired. Who does this?

NICK
Cambridge, Vermont

A Restoring your books will probably be a costly project. A book is grouped into "signatures," which are sewn together. They are usually from 10 to 20 pages. When a book starts to "shake," that is, the signature pages come loose from the bindings, the entire book has to be resewn with needle and thread, then reglued to the spine, which is the binding between the two covers. All of this has to be done by hand, so you can imagine how costly it is. Our local library sends its books to a book bindery in Boston. It is the Acme Book Binding, 100 Cambridge Street, Charlestown, MA 02129. You can also look in the yellow pages for a secondhand or antiquarian book dealer and ask for a book restoration person near you.

ENAMEL POT

Q I wonder if you can help me. I have a darling little enameled pot that my daughter brought to me from Italy. I've used it so much that now it has a pinhole in the bottom and it can't be used. Is there any way you know of to repair it?

E.D.H.
Proctor, Vermont

A Unfortunately, mending enameled pots is not safe. A drop of solder may hold for a while but it will be a fine breeding ground for bacteria. Since you enjoy this pot so much, why don't you find a liner, such as a plastic container, and use it for flowers?

CRIB MATTRESS AND WARNING

Q I've recently had my first baby. I found a nice oak crib for him before he was born. However, at the time I didn't know the federal government had standardized crib and mattress sizes. Hence my problem. I have an old mattress but it's not as firm as I would like. I need a size $47' \times 25'$. Except for buying a foam mattress and a new crib, I'm at a loss as to what to do.

D.P.
Randolph, Vermont

A Get a piece of plywood cut to fit your crib and then call an upholsterer and have him cut you a 4-inch piece of polystyrene. Ask him to cover it in mattress ticking or vinyl. A word of caution to all who have bought old or antique cribs for their babies: be sure the crib slats are no more than 2⅜ inches apart, so babies will not be able to slip through and be strangled. If the slats are farther apart, buy a bumper pad that runs around the inside of the entire crib. Be sure it can be securely tied or snapped into place. Bumper pads are a good idea in general. Cover all slats or rough edges with heavy tape. If the crib is more than twenty-five years old and is painted, it should be stripped and repainted, as the existing paint may contain dangerous levels of lead. Finally, be sure the mattress fits snugly. An infant can suffocate if it can wedge its head between the mattress and the crib. These are some of the problems with old cribs. Why don't you write for a free copy of "Crib Safety: Keep Them on the Safe Side," Product Safety Fact Sheet No. 43, from the U.S. Consumer Product Safety Commission, Washington, DC 20207.

DOWN COMFORTERS

Q I have a down comforter that has blown out—literally, the down is flying. It was a wedding present for my parents, who've been married fifty-nine years. In the

1950s it was recovered and now it needs more feathers and a new cover. Who provides this service?

FEATHERS FLYING
Northfield, Vermont

A The only place we know of that revitalizes comforters is The Company Store in La Crosse, Wisconsin. Call them at their toll-free number, 1-800-356-9367, and ask for their refurbishing service. They'll give you a rough estimate, as they can't be more specific until they see the comforter. They need to weigh the down and figure how much it will cost to take it apart. When they have seen the comforter, they'll send you a written estimate for the work. You can choose from several different styles and fabrics. You can even have your comforter turned into pillows. If you want to send your comforter directly, mail it to The Company Store, 2809 Losey Boulevard, La Crosse, WI 54601, Attn: Refurbishing.

Thanks to Virginia Dustin of Dustin Interior Design in Bondsville, we now know that right in Vermont there is a company that makes "the finest down comforters in the world!" Virginia enclosed a catalogue that tells all about the firm, its products, and the remake services it provides. She adds, "I have used their products and my clients have been so enthusiastic that they not only buy them for their homes up here on the mountain but have sent them to relatives, friends, and business acquaintances all over the world. Last week one even went off to China." For a free catalogue write to Down Under Company, Route 100, Weston, VT 05160.

READER FEEDBACK

IRON

ᗊᗕᗊᗕᗊᗕᗊᗕᗊᗕᗊᗕᗊᗕᗊᗕᗊᗕᗊᗕᗊᗕᗊᗕᗊᗕᗊᗕᗊᗕᗊᗕᗊᗕᗊᗕᗊᗕ

Q What can I do to a perfectly good steam iron that no longer steams? Is there a product available that could clear up this problem?

G.S.
Poultney, Vermont

A You probably have lime deposits clogging up your iron. Dear readers, do use distilled water in your steam irons. It will improve their longevity, especially where the water is hard. If there is any steam coming out of your iron at all, the following home remedy is about 90 percent effective. Fill your iron with white vinegar, plug it in, and set it either outside or in a well-ventilated area. Let it steam away until all the vinegar is gone, then rinse out. There are products for cleaning steam irons that you can buy in hardware stores, but they are expensive and don't work any better than the vinegar remedy. If no steam is coming out of your iron at all, we're afraid you're out of luck. It's just too badly clogged to be fixable.

MAYTAG DIRECTIONS

ᗊᗕᗊᗕᗊᗕᗊᗕᗊᗕᗊᗕᗊᗕᗊᗕᗊᗕᗊᗕᗊᗕᗊᗕᗊᗕᗊᗕᗊᗕᗊᗕᗊᗕᗊᗕᗊᗕ

Q When we moved into our new home in Chester last June, we acquired, among other things, a Maytag electric range. We have the installation instructions, but were not left the operating instructions and my wife needs to know how she can use the three back-panel controls. I wrote to what was identified in the telephone book as a Maytag appliance dealer in Brattleboro to no avail. Can you help us obtain the proper brochure?

W.F.B.
Chester, Vermont

A A couple of years ago, Nan had a problem with a Maytag appliance. She wrote to the company and received a prompt response. The address is: The Maytag Company, Newton, IA 50208. Their phone number is 515-792-7000.

RETINNING

Q I inherited some handsome copper pans but the tin inside them is worn. Do you know of a place that re-tins cookware?

P.T.M.
Brattleboro, Vermont

A There is a company in New York City called Re-Tinning and Copper Repair at 525 West 26th Street, New York, NY 10001 (212-244-4896) that does re-tinning, repairing, cleaning, and polishing of copper and tin. The Tinning Company at 69 Norman Street in Everett, MA 02149, also can solve your problem. Their phone is 617-389-3400.

UMBRELLA REPAIR

Q Do you know of anyone who can put new cloth covers on umbrellas? I have a large man's umbrella and it needs new black cloth only. All else is in good condition.

R.B.
Montpelier, Vermont

A We know of only one umbrella repair place; the day of disposables is upon us. It's Essex Umbrella Manufacturing Company, Endicott Street, Norwood, MA 02062 (617-770-2707). We published this info about a year ago, and the woman who had requested it kindly wrote to let us know that she had been delighted with the quality and efficiency of the Essex service.

WOODSTOVES

Q We own a Garrison woodstove which we bought over five years ago. At that time they sold repair kits to replace the firebrick on the inside of the stove. Since the store we bought the stove from is now closed and they don't make Garrison stoves anymore, is there anyplace where we could buy the kits or have the firebrick replaced?

M.N.
Springfield, Vermont

A Replacing firebrick in them is a challenge because of the octagonal shape of the Garrison stove. We've been unable to find the repair kits that you mention, and since Garrison has been out of business for four years, there are probably many Garrison owners searching for a solution to the same problem. We've come up with a couple of suggestions after talking to many people. The first is if there is anyone in your household who is able to use an electric circular saw, have that person buy a masonry blade and a pair of protective goggles. Buy standard firebrick and use the saw to cut bevels on the bricks that are required by the eight-sided stove. Another suggestion is that you buy standard firebrick and some Rutland Castable Refractory Cement. This product is described in the firm's brochure as follows: "Originally developed for use in blast furnaces, it has exceptional strength and abrasion resistance. It's ideal for replacing worn-out firebrick: the dry material is mixed with water, chemically sets, and dries brick hard. Can be cast into irregular shapes or as a solid bed." It seems to us that you could use this product for the beveled corner pieces where standard firebrick won't work or forget the bricks altogether and just use this product. If Rutland Products are not available at your local hardware store or stove dealership, call them toll-free to find out where to purchase their products, 1-800-222-6340 or 1-800-544-1307.

W.B. of Windsor, Vermont, kindly sent along a letter he received from Clifford Boran of the Midwest Antique Stove Information, Clearing House and Parts Registry. W.B. had written the Registry following a suggestion we made in the column when another reader asked if the Florence Stove Company was still in business. We know there's an interest in these stoves because of the number of letters we receive in reference to Florence stoves. Here's an abridged version of Mr. Boran's letter.

READER FEEDBACK

By our standards, your Florence range is decisively in the modern category and therefore outside the scope of our competence. We consider the antique era to have ended about 1935, when the first of the streamlined, chrome-trimmed white porcelain ranges began to appear. Florence stoves are named for Florence, Massachusetts. The company eventually moved to Gardner, Massachusetts, where your parts list shows they still had a factory even after the later move of the headquarters to Tennessee.... New England is Florence country and probably an especially good place to look for parts. Don't get your Florence Stove Company mixed up with the Florence Wood Coal Stoves made in Columbus, Ohio, by C. Emrich, which later became part of the George D. Roper Corporation. Possible sources for parts for kerosene ranges are: Lehman Hardware and Appliances, P.O. Box 41, Kidron, OH 44636 (this firm caters to the Amish community and specializes in nonelectric appliances); Macy's Texas Stove Works, 5515 Alameda Road, Houston, TX 77004 (a large and quite active gas range rebuilding shop, though the majority of their work is on 1940–1960 ranges). Dave Erickson is a very competent antique stove restorer-dealer who's knowledgeable about gas ranges as well as wood/coal burners. His address is P.O. Box 2275, Littleton, MA 01460.

STUCK STOPPER

Q I've a stuck stopper in a glass bottle which has a music box in the base. It's a German make, with pouring spout in cork. Should I soak it in something?

C.R.G.
Chelsea, Vermont

A Drop a little vegetable oil right where the stopper meets the bottle and let it sit overnight. Then carefully work the tip free. You may have to do this more than once.

WARPED RECORDS

Q My daughter borrowed one of my favorite records and returned it warped. Is there anything I can do to flatten it?

CRANKY MOM
Pomfret, Vermont

A Try this. (1) Take two sheets of ¼-inch plate glass 13 inches square. Make sure both the glass and the record are scrupulously clean. Any particles of dust that undergo the treatment will be imbedded forever in the delicate vinyl. (2)

Sandwich the record between the two sheets of glass. (3) Preheat the oven for about 15 minutes at the lowest possible setting. (4) Turn the oven off. (5) Place the record-and-glass sandwich on one of the oven racks and close the door. In about 15 minutes, open the oven door and let the sandwich cool in place. Complete cooling is important; half an hour is the minimum. If your oven is equipped with a pilot light, the normal oven ambient temperature might be sufficient for the baking process. In that case let the record sandwich cool out of the oven. Remember, it's always better to err on the safe side—too low a temperature for too short a time in the oven—than to overdo it. A record can always be treated again; a melted record is a total loss.

CHAPTER 6

WHERE CAN I FIND . . . ?

Do you want to find size 4 narrow shoes? sealing wax? or the S & H stamp redemption center? Perhaps a shield for chafing thighs, or how about a poem that includes the lines "I would rather have one flower, from the garden of a friend / Than a truckload of roses when my life on earth must end"? Maybe you're seeking a transcript of a TV show or a pair of ice grippers? These are the kind of questions that our readers pose, and if we can't find the answers, our dear readers almost always can.

POEM ABOUT A LADY WHO WORE PURPLE
∽∽

Q Would it be possible to get a copy of the poem about the lady who wore purple?

L.B.K.
Essex Junction, Vermont

A The name of the poem is "Warning" and it's by Jenny Joseph. Nan's father sent it to her in 1962 when it was first published in a British magazine called *The Listener*. Here is an excerpt.

Warning

When I am an old woman I shall wear purple
With a red hat which doesn't go, and doesn't suit me.
And I shall spend my pension on brandy and summer gloves.
And satin sandals, and say we've no money for butter.
I shall sit down on the pavement when I'm tired
And gobble up samples in shops and press alarm bells
And run my stick along the public railings
And make up for the sobriety of my youth.
I shall go out in my slippers in the rain
And pick the flowers in other people's gardens
And learn to spit.

You can wear terrible shirts and grow more fat
And eat three pounds of sausages at a go
Or only bread and pickle for a week
And hoard pens and pencils and beermats and things in boxes.

But now we must have clothes that keep us dry
And pay our rent and not swear in the street
And set a good example for the children.
We must have friends to dinner and read the papers.

But maybe I ought to practise a little now?
So people who know me are not too shocked and surprised
When suddenly I am old, and start to wear purple.

SNAPSHOT MADE INTO PICTURE POSTCARDS

Q I would like to know where to send a snapshot to be made into picture postcards. Also, where would I send a snapshot to be put onto notepaper?

MRS. E.D.M.
Barre, Vermont

A To have your snapshot made into a postcard, go to your nearest Kodak dealer and they'll make it into a black-and-white postcard; they don't do colored ones. For your notepaper go to a local printer. You can choose the color and quality of paper as well as the color of the ink.

SEALING WAX

Q Where can I buy sealing wax? I used to be able to get sealing wax sticks, scented, in various colors along with a little brass initial stamp. I can't find any replacements anywhere! Any suggestions?

M.H.
Woodstock, Vermont

A We were stumped, but reader A.W. of Proctor, Vermont, wrote, "Contact a jeweler who cuts and polishes his own stones. I think she might find the wax he uses on his dop stick to hold the gemstone in place while being polished could be used as sealing wax."

ICE GRIPPERS SO YOU WON'T SLIP

✉✉

Q Can you help me find a source of good grippers to wear with my shoes and boots in the icy parts of winter? Years ago, a neighbor who retired from the railroad noticed how I often fell down. He kindly gave me a pair of the grippers that the railway used to issue. After long, good service, they wore out. I bought would-be replacements from an army surplus store. These take forever to put on, their fittings are so complicated. They have spikes made for mountain climbing, so you must take them off before you get anywhere near any interior floor. I then tried the ones from a mail-order catalogue—these were plain elastic garters, which slip off when you're just walking along. I lost two pairs (four slip-offs!) in one winter. The good railroad kind had (and I hope still have) a belt that ran through two slats in a four-pointed cleat. You put the belt through a buckle, and if you got it tight enough, it would stay right all winter long. They inspired confidence, and didn't demand an engineering degree to use.

R.P.
Castleton, Vermont

A The Vermont Country Store in Weston, Vermont, carries "Never Slip Ice Safety Treads." According to the woman with whom we spoke, these grippers have four steel studs and are held on with strong rubber (like inner tube) straps. They cost $16.95. We called several sporting goods stores, and all we could come up with were grippers used by hikers. We were unable to reach anyone who works for a railroad. Dear readers, can you help us?

R.P. wrote again to tell us: "What a splendid network you have! Our Sunday paper came while I was out, somewhere around 8:30 A.M. Before either I or my wife got to your column, the phone rang. Here was a lady who wanted to sell me a pair of ice creepers (grippers) that didn't quite suit her and to tell me how to buy ones by mail like she did. I said I'd get back to her sometime this week. Mid-afternoon, I'm again out of the house; in comes the widow of our former town manager to give me a pair her husband used to wear. . . ."

READER FEEDBACK

ANAGLYPH

Q Could you please tell me where I can buy an *anaglyph*? Most places don't know what I'm talking about.

S.C.
Montpelier, Vermont

A Neither do we.

Our reply got us into a lot of hot water with our readers who felt (1) we had not done our job (we should have looked the word up in the dictionary) and (2) we were unnecessarily "curt" and "short." Sorry, S.C.! Anyway, J.F. and R.O. (among many others) said the *Webster's Heritage Dictionary* definition of an *anaglyph* was "(1) an ornament, as a cameo, carved in low relief, and (2) a photograph made up of two slightly different views, in contrasting colors, of the same subject, so that when looked at through a pair of corresponding color filters, the picture seems three-dimensional." Well, with all that information, we still didn't know what S.C. was looking for until we got this letter.

READER FEEDBACK

Q I don't believe it—the word is *anaglyph*—maybe I spelled it wrong. It's been called a cameo and is embedded in the ceiling as a base for chandeliers—a work of art. Thanks.

S.C.
Montpelier, Vermont

A We think your best bet is to buy a book called *Old House Journal Catalogue* published by Old House Journal. It comes out yearly and sells for $12.95. Another source for anaglyphs as well as ceiling medallions (we are still not sure which one you want) is Grinling, Ltd., 192 Christopher Columbus Drive, Jersey City, NJ 07302, a place that carries an extensive line of both items.

"DO NOT STAND BY MY GRAVE AND WEEP"

Q Please could you identify and complete this poem.

> Do not stand by my grave and weep
> I am not there, I do not sleep
> I am a thousand winds that blow
> I am a diamond glint on snow
> I am the sunlight on unripened grain
> I am the gentle autumn rain

M.F.
Perkinsville, Vermont

A

> When you awake in the morning hush
> I am the swift, uplifting rush
> Of quiet birds in circled flight.
> I am the soft stars that shine at night.
> Do not stand at my grave and cry;
> I am not there,
> I did not die.

Our mailbox was stuffed to the brim with the poem as it appears. M.F. of Springfield, Vermont, said she knows it as "A Prayer the Makah Indians Say," and A.D. of Rutland, Vermont, wrote: "On August 2, 1935, a beautiful man passed away. He was my grandfather. He left a void in the life of everyone who knew him. I was a teenager and a schoolmate sent me the enclosed poem. No title, no author. It was written just as I have copied it." The title of the poem is "Immortality," and we learned John Wayne recited it at the funeral of his friend, director Howard Hawks. It has since been published by Ann Landers, has appeared on a Shrine of La Salette prayer card, has been distributed by the Neptune Society for use in services for burial at sea, has been used by the Compassionate Society of Friends to comfort people on the death of a loved one, was read as a eulogy in a TV movie, and finally in 1986 won a second prize of $500 in a poetry contest sponsored by World of Poetry. Interestingly enough, this "anonymous" poem had been retitled "The Gentle Breeze" by the contestant, and was signed by his name, David Kellams.

RESOLUTION TRUST CORPORATION

Q I recently read about the U.S. government selling some $300 billion of assets from insolvent savings and loans. The name of the agency is the Resolution Trust Corporation. Could you find where to write or call to obtain information about these properties?

O.S.J.
Springfield, Vermont

A The Resolution Trust Corporation's address is 550 17th Street N.W., Washington, DC 20429, and the phone number is 202-789-6313.

FINDING A FINANCIAL ADVISOR

Q How does someone go about finding a financial advisor? I read in the paper about fast-talkers who are bilking elderly Vermonters out of their retirement money. How do you find someone who's honest?

JENNY
White River Junction, Vermont

A The Institute of Certified Financial Planners has a free questionnaire kit and booklet, "How to Select a Certified Financial Planner," which we think might be helpful as a starting point in your search for a planner. You might also ask your friends, lawyer, and/or banker for recommendations. Contact the Institute at 10065 East Harvard Avenue, Denver, CO 80231, for the questionnaire kit and booklet.

TRANSCRIPT OF TV SHOW

Q I used to work for Genisco Technology Corporation. A friend said he'd seen a story about the company on "60 Minutes" a week ago. Is there any way that I can get a transcript of the program?

GENE
Rutland, Vermont

A There is a company in New York City called Journal Graphics, at 269 Broadway, New York, NY 10007, that produces transcripts for a multitude of shows, including "60 Minutes." Telephone them at 212-227-7323 to order the transcript and charge it to your credit card or write them at the above address. The cost of the transcript you're seeking is $4.00. They also have topic lists (abortion, adoption, Africa, AIDS, etc.), which you may receive by sending a stamped, self-addressed envelope for up to five lists. For a book listing all of their topics, send $6.95.

S & H GREEN STAMP REDEMPTION

Q A neighbor told me that some time ago you gave an address for an S & H stamp redemption store, but I missed it, so if you know their location, please print it again. I wrote to the address listed in their books in Ohio, but the letter came back, so maybe they are out of business. I would appreciate your help as I have twenty-five books that I would like to redeem.

M.B.
Plainfield, Vermont

A There is no longer any place in either Vermont or New Hampshire where you can redeem your stamps. However, do not despair! S & H has a mail-order catalogue, which you can get by either calling 1-800-874-4438 or writing National Mail Order Center, The Sperry and Hutchinson Company, Inc., P.O. Box 5775, Norcross, GA 30091.

WOODSTOVE PARTS

Q Could you please send me the name and address of the place that makes or restores parts of the old Florence stoves?

M.N.
Rutland, Vermont

A As you know, The Florence Stove Company is no longer in business. Here are some possible sources for parts for your stove: Macy's Texas Stove Works, 5515 Alameda Road, Houston, TX 77004; Dave Erickson, P.O. Box 2275, Littleton, MA 01460; Midwest Antique Stove Information, Clearing House and Parts Registry, 417 North Main Street, Monticello, IN 47960. Be sure to send a stamped, self-addressed envelope when asking them about the parts or patterns to reproduce the parts. If you have to have the parts made, the Bryant Stove Works, in Thorn-dike, ME 04986 (207-568-3663), can do it.

"GIVE NOW"

Q We have a special occasion coming up in June and I would like to have the lines of a poem whose first lines are: "I would rather have one flower from the garden of a friend / Than a truckload of roses when my life on earth must end."

NO NAME
No town

A This verse is apparently a great favorite among our readers. We got a huge response! Our readers have it taped to refrigerators, fastened on cabinets, glued into Bibles, included in people's diaries, and inscribed in date books. A Baptist minister wrote that his copy was given him by a parishioner who wanted it read at the funeral of a family member. It is anonymous and variously entitled "Flowers Today," "Please Don't Wait," "One Little Rose," and "Give Now," among others.

I would rather have one little rose
From the garden of a friend
Than to have the choicest flowers
When my stay on earth must end.

I would rather have one pleasant word
In kindness said to me
Than flattery when my heart is still,
And life has ceased to be.

I would rather have a loving smile
From friends I know are true
Than tears shed 'round my casket,
When this world I bid adieu.

Blossoms bring to me today,
Whether pink or white or red;
I'd rather have one blossom now
Than a truckload when I'm dead.

HAMMER CRAFT COOKWARE REPLACEMENT HANDLES

Q For a good many years my favorite cooking pots have been a set of heavy hammered aluminum, but over the years the black handles have deteriorated, and I wonder if you can tell me where to obtain replacement handles if the company is still in business. On the bottom of the pans is stamped "Hammer Craft Cookware" with a sort of four-leaf clover with the words "Hammered Club Aluminum."

J.R.
Barre, Vermont

A Hammer Craft was made by Regal Cookware, which is still very much in business. You can order replacement handles for your Hammer Craft set by writing Regal Cookware, Attn: Consumer Service, 1675 Reigle Drive, Kewaskum, WI 53040. The handles are $2 each plus $2 handling charge for the order. The order number for the handles is AX 2771. When you order, be sure to specify that you want the black rather than the wooden handles, which came on Hammer Craft that was manufactured twenty years ago or more.

DURABLE RUBBER FLOOR TILE

Q We have inquired and searched for durable tile for a farm kitchen floor—so far no luck. Reading your column faithfully, it seems your knack of "search and find" is unique. We have some rubber tile without mark or cracks after twenty-seven years' wear. Now we are told it is not available. Is there any hope of finding some, or its equal? The answer we get is that durability is not a quality promoted today.

O.C.
Fair Haven, Vermont

A The closest we could get to your now unavailable rubber tile is a tile called Radial Rubber Tile, which not only is as long-lasting and durable as your old kind but, because of the way it holds the adhesive, is actually better. It is a little thicker than the old rubber tile and comes in large squares; the smallest dimension is 18 inches. It's made by Johnsonite, Mono and Armstrong, and other manufacturers.

INFO ON OLD MOVIES

Q What and where is the best source for obtaining info on old movies? Having been a movie buff most of my life, I am most curious about facts concerning films seen almost seventy years ago.

R.G.G.
Woodstock, Vermont

A Three excellent sources that can be found in the reference section of most libraries are *The Film Encyclopedia* by Ephraim Katz, *The Biographical Dictionary of Film* by David Thomson and *Halliwell's Filmgoer's Companion,* Ninth Edition (1988).

CLOTH DIAPERS WITH VELCRO CLOSINGS

Q About three months ago I received an ad to purchase cloth diapers. These were folded like disposable, had plastic pants already attached to them, and had Velcro closings instead of pins. I didn't need them then and threw out the ad. I would really like to locate them now.

L.T.
White River Junction, Vermont

A The diapers, or Bio-Bottoms, you are looking for are available from Seventh Generation, a mail-order company that specializes in ecologically beneficial products. It is located in Burlington, Vermont. For a catalogue call them toll-free at 1-800-456-1177.

LIQUID BLUING

Q Please tell me where I can find liquid bluing. *The Museum of Science Magazine* in Boston has put out directions for making snow crystals and magic crystals (to make a snow-covered tree). The crystal solution requires table salt, water, liquid bluing, and ammonia. The "tree" is of green blotting paper or construction paper. I had thought some older person might have some bluing tucked away, but no luck, and the local stores don't carry it.

G.S.
Pawlet, Vermont

A Sawyer's Liquid Bluing is available in many grocery stores in the laundry section. If you can't find it locally, write Luther Ford and Company, the distributor, at Box 201405, Bloomington, MN 55420.

LINEN TOWELING

Q I am looking for linen crash about 20 inches by 22 inches wide. Remember the old-fashioned roller towels that hung on the wall? They usually had a red or blue border trim.

F.M.M.
East Corinth, Vermont

A The Vermont Country Store in Weston, Vermont, carries the linen crash that you're seeking. It comes with red, yellow, green, or red stripes and costs $3.60 a yard. For specifics call them at 802-362-2400 or write them at P.O. Box 3000, Manchester Center, VT 05255-3000.

LOUD ALARM CLOCK

Q I am looking for a loud alarm clock. I work nights, do not get a lot of sleep, and have trouble waking up to go to work. I cannot find a clock loud enough to wake me.

T.E.
Springfield, Vermont

A Try placing your current alarm clock (this won't work if it's part of a digital radio; you need a real alarm clock) in a metal baking dish. We don't think you'll have any problems waking up. This little trick will amplify your alarm to a point that approaches your pain threshold.

S.R. of Plainfield, Vermont, and G.M. of East Calais, Vermont, wrote to suggest that T.E. get a clock radio. G.M.'s son has a hearing problem and S.R.'s daughter is a sound snoozer, and both report that a clock radio with the volume turned up works for wake-ups.

READER FEEDBACK

SHOES FOR TINY FEET

Q I can't find any store in Barre or in the Burlington area that sells dress shoes in size 2½ or 3. I have worn size 5 for years, but my feet have shrunk.

VINNIE
Barre, Vermont

A We know of two places that carry shoes in the sizes you're seeking, and both publish catalogues. The first is Cinderella of Boston, Inc., P.O. Box 71100, Canoga Park, CA 91304, and the second is Hill Brothers, 99 Ninth Street, Lynchburg, VA 24504. They carry over six hundred styles of only women's shoes in widths from AAAA to EEEE.

SHOES FOR EXTRA-WIDE FEET

Q Do you know of any shoe outlet that specializes in women's shoes in extra-wide widths?

S.A.
Montpelier, Vermont

A P. L. Premium Leather by Hanover, P.O. Box 340, Hanover, PA 17331, carries shoes from AA to EEE in sizes 6–15. Hill Brothers, mentioned in the preceding answer, also carries shoes in wide widths.

LONG HAIRPINS

Q Can you help me locate hairpins? Not the flimsy inadequate ones available in local department stores but the good old-fashioned ones that were 2 to 2½ inches long, made of a heavier wire. I also used to use tortoiseshell hairpins and I have not been able to locate those either.

N.L.
Rutland, Vermont

A The Vermont Country Store carries the pins you're seeking. For $10.80 you get one dozen Faux-Tortoise hairpins. They're faux because it's illegal to import tortoiseshell in the U.S. because of the endangered species law. They also carry Jumbo (3-inch) metal hairpins. Their catalogue, *Voice of the Mountains*, is available by writing P.O. Box 3000, Manchester Center, VT 05255-3000.

REVERE WARE REPLACEMENTS

Q Could you locate the address for Revere Ware copper-bottom pans—two covers have disappeared and need replacing.

I.B.
Stratton Mountain, Vermont

A The address you want is Revere Ware Customer Service, P.O. Box 250, Clinton, IL 16127.

PEN PAL

Q My daughter is looking for a pen pal from another state or country. Do you know where she could get a listing of people who would be willing to be pen pals?

LORI
Montpelier, Vermont

A There is an organization called the Student Letter Exchange at 215 Fifth Avenue S.E., Waseca, MN 56093, whose purpose is "to build better international goodwill through pen pal correspondence between young people ages 10–19 in the U.S. and other countries." All correspondence is in English.

PEN PALS FOR WIDOWS, WIDOWERS, AND CATHOLICS

Q I am interested in finding out if there is such a thing as a pen pal club for widows, widowers, or a Catholic pen pal club.

MRS. V.D.
Rutland, Vermont

A There is a Friendship Club, written about in the *Catholic Golden Age Magazine*, which is available free from a Catholic church. If you are a golden-ager you could send your name to Rita Howell at 4000 Greenwood Boulevard, Harrisburg, PA 17109; she is in charge of the club. If you would like a pen pal in a foreign country, write to the International Friendship League at 22 Batterymarch Street, Boston, MA 02109. This is an international correspondence society with one million members. It was founded in 1948 and matches Americans with pen pals in 139 countries and territories.

WOODEN STRIKE-ANYWHERE MATCHES

Q Would you know where a person could get the old wooden (strike-anywhere) matches? The only ones I can find in area stores are strike-on-the-box types.

R.M.
Worcester, Vermont

A Strike-anywhere matches are available from Diamond Brands Inc. A case of 48 boxes costs $24.65 and includes shipping. The product code is 02122. To send for them, write Customer Service, Diamond Brands Inc., 1804 Cloquet Avenue, Cloquet, MN 55720, and enclose a check or money order.

THIGH SHIELD

Q I'm a big woman and have a problem with my thighs rubbing together. I've heard there's some kind of a shield you can buy to help with this problem. Do you have any idea where I can get one?

BIG
Montpelier, Vermont

A We found just what you're looking for in *Voice of the Mountains*, the Vermont Country Store catalogue. It's a contraption called a Chafing Shield and consists of a strap that goes around the waist, attached to two straps that go down the side and connect to a pair of shields that are held between the thighs with another pair of elastic straps. The address for the catalogue is P.O. Box 3000, Manchester Center, VT 05255-3000.

STOP UNWANTED MAIL

Q I am sick to death of the pounds of catalogues that I receive in the mail. How can I stop them from coming?

ENOUGH ALREADY
Proctor, Vermont

A Write to: Direct Marketing Association, 11 West 42nd Street, New York, NY 10036. Include all the names or initials on the catalogues that come to you. You also might call the companies that have 800 numbers—this costs them and not you—and ask to be taken off their mailing lists.

DEHUMIDIFIER KNOBS

Q I've looked everywhere—well, almost—for food dehumidifiers—a knob filled with blue crystals that absorbs humidity in crackers (or whatever) and turns pinkish. You bake it and it dries out and can be used again and again. I've seen them available as just the knob, or the knob on top of a cracker can. I can't find either and I've been looking for two years.

M.C.
Montpelier, Vermont

A We couldn't find your knob dehumidifiers either, but think you can jury-rig something similar. The blue stuff that turns pink is nothing more or less than silica gel, a drying agent used primarily for drying flowers. You can buy it at craft stores, general stores, and nurseries that also carry a range of gardening supplies. Take a square piece of cloth, pour some of the silica gel in the center, tie the cloth with a string (much as you would a sachet), and drop the little packet in your cracker tin or cookie jar. When the gel turns pink, put it in the oven at 250 degrees until it turns blue once again.

R.B.B. of Manchester Center, Vermont, wrote to tell us the product M.C. is looking for is called Blue Magic and is manufactured by the Luce Corporation. "I was secretary to the president of the company when it was started back in the late 1940s, so I know a little bit about the product," she said. Write to The Luce Corporation, 336 Putnam Avenue, P.O. Box 4124, Hamden, CT 06514. These knobs are also available from L. L. Bean in Freeport, ME.

READER FEEDBACK

HISTORICAL CLOTHING

Q I'm curious about what people wore two hundred years ago. I imagine it was practical and long-wearing. How could I find out more about it and perhaps find some patterns?

J.H.
Rutland, Vermont

A A recently published book, *Put on Thy Beautiful Garments: Rural New England Clothing, 1783–1800*, by Meredith Wright of Montpelier, Vermont, should meet your needs. Reproductions of the clothes described in the book can be made by using pattern diagrams, instructions, and resources included in the book. You can order your copy by sending a check for $12.50 plus $3.00 for postage and handling to The Clothes Press, P.O. Box 686, Montpelier, VT 05601-0686.

WESTERN-STYLE SHIRT COLLAR TIPS

Q Would you or your readers know where I can obtain western-style shirt collar tips? I have been looking everywhere but I haven't been able to find any.

P.B.
Barre, Vermont

A We couldn't answer this, but our readers sent us several sources. The two most frequently mentioned are Sheplers in Wichita, Kansas (1-800-833-7007), and Cheyenne Outfitters in Wyoming (1-800-234-0432).

REPLACEMENT SILVER TOPS FOR SALT AND PEPPER SHAKERS

Q I would like to replace the silver tops on a pair of small crystal salt and pepper shakers which are of sentimental value. I have tried jewelry stores and gift shops but have had no luck.

W.S.
Montpelier, Vermont

A Our answer is thanks to reader R.T. of Meriden, Connecticut. "Tell her to write to J. C. Boardman Company, Hartford Turnpike South, Wallingford, CT 06492. They make pewter tops and silver-plated tops for all sizes of salt and pepper shakers (very reasonable prices) and they make a thousand other items too! I retired from Boardman after sixteen years," R.T. wrote.

WOOL FROM YOUR OWN FLEECE

Q We have some friends who raise sheep. They would like to have some yarn spun from their own fleece. They have been unable to find any place that will return their very own wool to them—apparently it always get mixed with other people's. Do you know anyone who can spin their wool for them?

S.H.
Philadelphia, Pennsylvania

A The Green Mountain Spinnery in Dummerston, Vermont, fills this very niche in the yarn-manufacturing market, as the firm focuses on the small sheep breeder. They will custom-process wool as long as you have at least 100 pounds of fleece. The fleece must be clean and free of chaff, burrs, and tags. It should be stored dry, preferably in burlap bags. Fleeces from white-face, black-face, and colored sheep should be kept separate, since each is used to produce different kinds of yarn. They can blend your wool with their own natural dyed wools, which results in heathers. They also offer precious fiber blends by mixing wool with mohair and Angora rabbit. This company also sells Vermont designer kits and knitting patterns for a multitude of sweaters, as well as mittens and socks. For more information or a catalogue, write to Green Mountain Spinnery, Box 568, Putney, VT 05346. Their toll-free number is 1-800-321-WOOL (9665).

CHAPTER 7

WHAT'S IT WORTH?

New Englanders tend to squirrel things away. We have attics, cellars, barns, and sheds, and we tend to fill them all. Old tools, books, records, and clothing are just some of the items we hang on to; when we get ready to dig out, we often have yard sales or auctions. These events we enjoy as social occasions as well as a prime opportunity to acquire some more stuff. What's it worth? our readers ask us, and we are often surprised. We expect you will be too.

ANTIQUE BUTTON COLLECTION

Q Could you tell me where I could get information and/or appraisal of a large antique button collection?

M.P.
Enfield, New Hampshire

A There is a National Button Society to which you can write for the name and address of a certified button appraiser near you. Write to them at 2733 Juno Place, Akron, OH 44333.

BELLS

Q I have two bells. The biggest is 3½ inches tall and 4 inches across the bottom. The smaller one is 2½ inches tall and 3 inches across the bottom. On one side is a date of 1878 and on either side of the date is an emblem that looks like a cross and beneath this is a word, *Saignelegier*. On the other side of the bells are these words, one above the other, *Chiantel/Fondeur*. There are emblems or symbols around the top above the words. They appear to be circles, but are quite worn. Everything on the bells, i.e., year, lettering, etc., is raised. Both bells are the same. We have a farm that has been in the family for years. We found them in a building here about five years ago. I have been to the library and couldn't find out anything.

G.S.
West Rupert, Vermont

A We'll bet you dollars to doughnuts that what you have are two Swiss cowbells. In the spring Swiss farmers herd all their cows together, communally, and send them into upper Alpine pastures. Each cow is belled so that in the fall, when they are brought down, each farmer can claim his own cow. The cross is the Helvetian (or Swiss) symbol. Saignelegier is probably the name of the farmer, and Chiantel Fondeur is the name of either his village or his farm. The lettering is raised because embossing lasts longer than engraving. The emblems or symbols around the tip are worn because that is where the bell rests closest against the neck of the cow. Anne, whose father used to live in Switzerland, remembers going up into the high Alpine meadows of a summer's evening and hearing the bells, each one with a different tone, sounding through the mountains. The date is, we assume, the date of the manufacture of the bells.

BARBIE DOLLS

Q I just recently heard on TV that the original Barbie Doll is now worth about $1,000—so having found my girls had an original, I would now like to know where to sell it.

M.E.B.
Bellows Falls, Vermont

A For the original Barbie Doll to be worth $1,000, it has to meet four criteria. First, it really does have to be original, i.e., the first lot made. Second, it has to be in its original box. If it is not, the value drops to about $500. Third, it must be in mint condition, never played with; and fourth, you have to find someone who wants to buy it! For more information, see if your library has either *Barbie Dolls* by Susan Paris and Carlos Manos, published by Collectors Books in 1982, or *The World of Barbie Dolls* by the same authors, which was also published by Collectors Books, in 1983.

KEWPIE DOLLS

Q Kewpie dolls are a collector's item as well as a part of our American folklore. Rose O'Neill of Branson, Missouri, wrote and illustrated Kewpic children's stories in 1909. Then she created the Kewpie doll, which first appeared in 1913. So popular were her Kewpies that after her death in 1944, a plaque identifying her home was erected by a group of doll enthusiasts. Collecting has gone on ever since. I would like to know what value to place on Rose O'Neill's 2¼-inch tiny blue winger Kewpie, marked with a topknot. Can you tell me the value?

M.W.
Montpelier, Vermont

A Your Kewpie is worth $85–$95, according to *Seventh Blue Book Dolls & Values*, Hobby House Press, Inc., 1983.

BOOKS

Q I have a book, *Andrew Wyeth* by Richard Merryman. It's a large book, 13 inches by 17½ inches. It is a first printing, copyright 1968 by Houghton Mifflin Company, Boston. Can you tell me its value and also where I can find a purchaser?

LYDIA
Proctorsville, Vermont

A If the book still has its dust jacket and is in absolutely mint condition, it is probably worth about $80 if you sold it to a book dealer. If you sold it yourself, you might get up to $100, but in order to do that you'd have to find someone who wanted to buy it. If you have a copy that is part of a limited edition (it will say so on one of the pages before the title page, giving number of volumes in the edition and the number of your volume), it is considerably more valuable.

Here are a few criteria to follow to help you decide if a book is of any value to a book collector. Any one of these either alone or in combination is to be considered. (1) A book must be rare (i.e., very few printed or very few still in circulation); (2) it must be something that is in demand (*The Authentic Life of President McKinley*, for example, is not); (3) the book may be "autographed," i.e., signed by the author, or even better, be a presentation volume (i.e., have a handwritten inscription by the author to a particular person); and (4) the book may be a first edition, if first editions of that author's book have become rare or are unique in some way. For instance, a first edition of Louisa May Alcott's *Little Women* is worth quite a lot of money because, unlike later editions, it is printed in one part, or volume, only. The second edition was published with Part 2 added, and that is how the book has continued to appear. Check the yellow pages to find a book dealer in your area.

CIGAR BANDS

Q I am a retired banker anxious to find out whether or not you know of anyone who collects or has a cigar-band collection. I have three books filled with over one thousand cigar bands (very colorful), accumulated since the early 1930s.

Most of the companies who made cigars or printed cigar bands are now defunct. I would like to meet anyone who could add to my collection. Do you think this collection has any value?

M.R.
Rutland, Vermont

A Cigars enjoyed enormous popularity between 1880 and 1930. By 1940 they had been outstripped by cigarettes. We don't know what the value of your collection is, but for $6.50 a year you can join the International Seal, Label and Cigar Band Society, 1985 East Bellevue Street, Tucson, AZ 85715. This collector's club can certainly help you with the value of your collection as well as suggest ways to add to it. You also might write "Tobacco Bill" Hatcher, 713 Parrott Avenue,

M.R. later brought us up to date: "Back in 1988 you did some investigative work for me. It relaunched my hobby having started back in the 1930s. The references you gave me then started me on a voyage which, much to my joy, may not end until I become permanently incapacitated. Since our correspondence began, my collection has more than doubled, and I have made new friends in the cigar-band business, both as retailers and as hobbyists. So far I have had my own feedback from Pennsylvania, Connecticut, Florida, Puerto Rico, Ohio, and Arizona. My happiest connection is with a Mr. Hruby, age seventy-eight, from Ohio, who is in the *Guinness Book of Records* and how! I want to thank you for your assistance just when I was searching for something to occupy my leisure hours."

READER FEEDBACK

Kingston, NC 28501. He's a collector of all tobacco items, products, packages, books, literature, bill heads, tins, premiums, etc., and David Freiberg, Cerebro Lithographers, Box 1221, Lancaster, PA 17603. He's a dealer in cigar box labels, fruit crate labels, and general tobacco ephemera such as cigar bands and cigarette cards.

TOKEN

Q We have been unable to find much information regarding a coin we have. On one side around the edge, it says, "Free Soil, Free Speech John O. Fremont," and there is a head of, presumably, Mr. Fremont in the middle. On the other side is the American eagle symbol and around the edge it says, "United States of America." There is no date. As far as we know, Fremont was a man who led the settlers out west.

M.R.
Rutland, Vermont

A What you have is one of the campaign tokens Mr. Fremont handed out to his constituents when he was running for President in 1857. These tokens were very popular with political candidates in the 1830s through the 1880s and frequently had a hole punched near the top so they could be worn on a watch fob. Depending on its condition, your token is worth anywhere from $24 to $40.

COINS

Q I am interested in knowing the sale value of Indian head pennies dated from1902, 1903, and 1907 in excellent condition. The local appraisers vary a lot. I also have a mint-condition gold quarter-dollar, with no date. Again local dealers vary, so I am wondering just what the value is.

S.M.
Montpelier, Vermont

A As we've so often reminded our readers, the value of an item depends on how much people are willing to pay for it. From coins to cars, there is very often a published book value; then you have to get someone to agree that's how much they'll pay. A dealer will pay less because he has to make a profit at resale. The book value for your pennies is 30 cents each. You didn't give us enough of a description of the gold piece for us to go on. It could be worth anywhere from $40 to $300.

MEDAL

Q Some time ago my son found a medal with a ship on one side with *U.S. Frigate Constellation* inscribed above it and the date *1792* below it. On the other side is an eagle above the words *This coin struck from parts of the Frigate Constellation, The First Ship of the U.S. Navy*, between what might be two cannons. Can you tell me if this medal has any value?

A.S.
Sudbury, Vermont

Ⓐ While the waterfront was being revitalized in Baltimore, a group formed to restore the *Constellation*, which at that time was just a hulk floating in the harbor. To raise money, coins were struck using the copper from the hull of the ship. The only value of the coin is that it provides free admission for a tour of the ship.

MINT SET

Ⓠ Could you give me an idea of what a mint set would be worth to a collector and do you know of an interested party? I have mint sets dating from 1933 to 1973.

BILL
Montpelier, Vermont

Ⓐ The U.S. Mint didn't start producing mint sets until 1947, so the chances are that what you have, at least up to 1947, are "year sets" that someone put together. If you have an original mint set from 1947, it's worth from $550 to $600; the prices go down from there, although the 1949 set is worth between $450 and $500 because of low mintage that year. By 1960 the mint was printing so many sets that the value plummeted. The sets are worth, from 1960 on, $6 to $10.

SILVER CERTIFICATES

Q Are either of you numismatically inclined? I have a set of one hundred U.S.A. Silver Certificates, $1 each, Series 199935-F Priest-Anderson, Blue Sea UNC, with consecutive serial numbers R 9450800-I through R 94508100-I, inclusive. They are in what I call "good" condition, slightly handled but not used. About like what the bank hands over when you ask for new bills. I also have a treasury note ("Assistant Secretary of the United States, Albany, N.Y."). It has an imprint of William McKinley, made out to Wilson Clothing Company of Rutland, Vermont, in 1911 for a pair of fishing boots. It was never cashed but instead was framed. Why? I've no idea. The amount was for $5. It is stamped with a six-digit number and signed by a "Disbursing Clerk," whose signature is undecipherable.

R.G.W.
Woodstock, Vermont

A Although neither of us is numismatically inclined and we seem to spend our money faster than we can collect it, we do have a great resource in the Barre Coin and Hobby Shop in Barre, Vermont. Your silver certificates are worth $1.75 wholesale and $2.25 to $2.50 retail.

NAZI FLAG

Q I was given a Nazi flag. It was captured in Germany at the end of WW II. Would you be able to tell me how much it is worth? The flag is in excellent shape.

L.B.
Cuttingsville, Vermont

A The flag is probably a party flag, one of the hundreds of thousands of flags manufactured during Hitler's regime, to be displayed outside Nazi homes or waved during parades and rallies of the faithful. Because there are so many around, they are not in great demand. Your flag is worth about $30.

GERMAN ARMY OFFICER'S SWORD

Q I have a German Army officer's sword which someone has asked me to sell to them. I have no idea of the value or where to ask about the value. It has the name *Solingen* on the sword, an embedded brass swastika in the hilt, and it is in a leather case with a brass trim and a brass tip.

V.M.H.
Randolph, Vermont

A Our military-collectibles dealer says your sword is worth $100 to $150. It's best to take your sword to a dealer, as they are able to give more accurate estimates if they can see the item. To find a military-collectibles dealer, ask a local antique dealer or gun dealer.

ELVIS PRESLEY LETTERS

Q I was wondering if there was an Elvis Presley Memorabilia Club. If so, what is the address? I have a couple of letters in his handwriting which I've been told are valuable and therefore could be sold or auctioned.

A FAN
Hardwick, Vermont

A We went right to the source, as it were, and called Graceland in Memphis, Tennessee. The very pleasant lady we spoke with told us that the Elvis Presley Museum doesn't buy any Elvis letters because they are impossible to authenticate. "Just about everyone seems to have something Elvis owned, or touched, or wrote," she said, "and it's just about impossible to tell the real from the fake, so we just don't get involved in that." However, she did say that they would be willing to authenticate his signature for you, and if it proves to be authentic, you could put an ad in their newsletter, *Graceland Express*, which is subscribed to by Elvis memorabilia collectors and fans throughout the country. If you are interested in getting the signatures on the letters authenticated, write to Communications Department, P.O. Box 16508, Memphis, TN 03816-0508, Attn: Patsy

Anderson. They'll send you the particulars of how to go about sending your letters down. If you'd rather skip that step and just go ahead and place an ad in *Graceland Express*, write to the above address, Attn: *Graceland Express*, and request the necessary information.

RECORDS

◁▽

Q   Do you know of anyone that collects or is interested in the old 78 rpm phonograph records? I have about fifteen albums of famous entertainers such as Sinatra, Como, Lombardo, etc.

L.H.
South Barre, Vermont

A   As a rule of thumb, 78's are about as valuable as yesterday's newspaper. Most of the "classic" popular recordings have been rerecorded, remastered, and reissued on 33's or compact discs. If you are curious to find the value of your records, there is a wonderful reference book called *American Premium Guide, Third Edition (1915–65)*, published by Books Americana and distributed by Charles Tuttle, Rutland, Vermont, for $14.95. It is not only an encyclopedic compendium of record identification and values, but contains a section on where to buy, sell, or trade records. If you don't want to spring for the $14.95, look in the reference section of your public library or ask your librarian to obtain the book for you through the interlibrary loan system.

AUTHENTICATION OF ANTIQUE SIGNATURE

Q Is there anyplace in New England where one can get an antique signature authenticated? A friend has a notebook that might have some writing by and signed by one of our late great presidents. She would like to have it seen and validated if it is his signature.

M.A.M.
Barre, Vermont

A One of the most reputable signature experts on the East Coast is a gentleman by the name of Kenneth Rendell. His address is 154 Wells Avenue, Newton, MA 02159. He has an 800 number: 1-800-447-1007. You can call and discuss the matter with him.

FRANKLIN MINT PLATES

Q I have six Franklin Mint plates: four Woodland series ($65 each), one Christmas plate, 24-carat gold edging ($125), and one Mother's Day Flower plate ($65). Could you tell me where I could sell these plates?

AN EX-COLLECTOR
White River Junction, Vermont

A As we have often advised our readers, the value of a "collectible" object is determined by two factors, the demand for it and the rarity of the object. For instance, a collectible can be quite rare, but if no one wants to buy it, it isn't worth much. Although Franklin Mint plates are advertised as collectibles, they are manufactured in fairly large quantities; many of the collector series plates are issued in lots of twelve thousand or more. Eventually they will probably be worth more than they are now, but in the books we consulted, none of the plates you have listed has increased in value by more than $1, and that is if you were to sell them yourself. If you were to take them to a dealer, he or she would probably pay you somewhat less than your original purchase price, as, obviously, the dealer would have to make a profit on the resale. We suggest you hang on to the plates for a while.

KOOL CIGARETTE PENGUINS

Q I have a set of Millie and Willie, the Kool cigarette penguins. They are plastic salt and pepper shakers made by F and F Mold and Dye Works, Dayton, Ohio. Are they worth anything? How much?

K.W.
Mount Holly, Vermont

A Millie and Willie are worth about $8 to $10. At the moment, there are lots of Millies and Willies still around and Kool cigarettes are still on the market, but who knows what the future will bring? Why don't you tuck them carefully away and maybe in ten years they'll be worth something.

FIESTAWARE

Q I am looking for someone who can tell me the value of Fiestaware, thirty to forty years old.

C.F.
Montpelier, Vermont

A There's a book called *The Collector's Encyclopedia of Fiestaware* by Bob and Sharon Huxford. It can be ordered from the publisher, Collector Books, P.O. Box 3009, Paducah, KY 42001. The price is $19.95 with an additional postage and handling charge of $1. It's a lively compendium of information on Fiestaware, of which there are a great many types and patterns. It also lists the value of the pieces. You can also find a limited listing on Fiestaware in many of the books on collectibles such as *Warman's Americana and Collectibles* and *Kovels' Antiques and Collectibles Price List*.

HUMMEL

ᴍᴍ

Q I have a sizable Hummel figurine collection that I would like to dispose of. Could you please advise me as to the best method of doing this? I would like to sell the collection in its entirety, not one piece at a time.

MAMIE
South Barre, Vermont

A Trot over to your nearest bookstore or library and find a copy of *Luckey's Hummel Figurines and Plates, Sixth Edition*, published by Books Americana and distributed by Charles Tuttle, Rutland, Vermont. On page 61, there is a listing of Hummel publications and newsletters throughout the country. You can doubtless sell your collection by advertising in one or all of these.

OCCUPIED JAPAN PLAQUES

ᴍᴍ

Q I have two porcelain (I'm not sure of that) wall plaques of a colonial man and woman. The backs of the items say, "Occupied Japan." Do you think they have any value? I know they are quite old, as I got them from my grandmother and she had them for years.

K.S.P.
Castleton, Vermont

A Your plaques are highly collectible and worth about $40 a pair. There is an Occupied Japan Club. Send a stamped, self-addressed envelope in care of Florence Archambault, 29 Freedom Street, Newport, RI 02840, for more information.

CHAPTER 8

RECIPE REQUESTS AND FOOD FACTS

Our readers ask us for recipes that run the gamut from sweet to sour, soup to nuts. Requests for pickles, cookies, breads, and soups have in recent years outnumbered the recipes that call for marshmallows and packaged cake mix. Many of the requests we receive reflect the seasons. Be it how to crack butternuts, how to fry tripe so it's brown, or how to concoct Needhams (candy that includes mashed potatoes, paraffin, and coconut), our readers' requests are rarely dull.

WINTER PEAR BISQUE

Q I recently had dinner at The Inn at Long Last in Chester, Vermont. While the entire meal was delicious, the Winter Pear Bisque was memorable. Can you find me a recipe for this wonderful soup?

D.G.
Woodstock, Vermont

A We couldn't find the recipe anywhere, so phoned up Jack Coleman, the proprietor of The Inn at Long Last, and asked if he would be so kind as to send the recipe to us, which he forthwith did. The recipe was sent courtesy of Chef Michael Williams.

2 ounces peanut oil
1 medium onion, diced
12 pears, peeled, cored, and chopped
1 quart chicken stock
2 cups pear fruit wine
2 large sprigs rosemary
2 cinnamon sticks
2 cups heavy cream

Sauté onions in oil until sweated. Add pears, cook 10 minutes. Add wine and reduce by half. Cover with stock and spices, bring to a boil. Reduce and simmer for 20 minutes. Remove rosemary sprigs and cinnamon sticks. Puree soup in food processor. Return to heat with cream and season to taste with a dollop of crème fraîche.

CRÈME FRAÎCHE

Q I love reading recipes in magazines and newspapers. Recently I have come across an ingredient called "crème fraîche." If my high school French serves, that translates into fresh cream. Is it? If not, what is it and where do you get it?

M.N.
Hartland, Vermont

A Your high school French is a little bit off. You are right that *crème* is "cream" in translation; however, *fraîche* means "in the cool of the day." "Cream in the cool of the day" apparently makes little sense, but like many French things, is, in the final analysis, sensible. The old way of making crème fraîche was to leave cream sitting out for a day and then, in the evening, to skim off the top, which was then refrigerated. The way it's made now is to whisk together 1 cup of heavy cream (make sure it's not the ultrapasteurized variety) and 1 cup of sour cream, cover and let sit out all day, overnight, or until thickened. Cover and refrigerate for at least 4 hours, after which the crème fraîche will be even thicker. What you end up with is an extremely hearty, rather tart, absolutely delicious cream which is perfect for berries, and as a replacement for sour cream in sauces, soups, and gravies. Unlike sour cream, it does not separate and "melt" when heated.

FRUIT SOUFFLÉ

Q I'd like to make a fresh fruit soufflé but I can't find a recipe. Could you please help?

S.T.
Rutland, Vermont

A Fruit soufflés are simple as can be. First you need to make a fruit puree. Use about ½ pound of fruit. Peel, chop, and cook if it's hard. Then put it in a food processor or blender.

¾ cup fruit puree
1 tablespoon lemon juice
pinch of salt
sugar to taste
3 egg whites

Butter a 1-quart soufflé dish and sprinkle with sugar. Heat the puree. Add juice, sugar, salt. Remove from heat. Beat egg whites until stiff and stir into the warm puree until blended. Pour into prepared dish. Bake at 375 degrees for 20–25 minutes. This will serve four.

HOMEMADE SALAMI

Q I've heard there's an easy way to make salami, but I haven't been able to find a recipe. Do you or your readers have any ideas?

T.M.
Wallingford, Vermont

A Nan was given this recipe by her husband's aunt, Carolyn Emsch of Rittman, Ohio, and it's terrific.

5 pounds hamburger
4 tablespoons curing salt (Nan uses Morton's Tender Quick)

2½ teaspoons Liquid Smoke
1 teaspoon garlic salt
2½ teaspoons coarsely ground pepper
2½ teaspoons mustard

Knead all ingredients together and put in a large bowl, cover, and put in the fridge. Knead five minutes each day for four days. On the fourth day, after kneading, shape into five or six rolls. Place on a rack over a cookie sheet or use a large broiler pan to catch the drippings. Bake 9 hours at 160 degrees. Turn the rolls a few times during the baking process. Store in the fridge or freeze.

PIG HILL PASTA

1 pound pasta—fresh is a real treat
4 cloves garlic, chopped
4 tablespoons melted butter
4 tablespoons olive oil
1 cup parsley, chopped
¼ pound extra sharp cheddar cheese, grated or shredded

Chop garlic. Add to melted butter and olive oil. Sauté slowly for 10 minutes, then add parsley. Cook pasta, add garlic/parsley mixture and cheese. Toss and serve.

DEAR ANNE AND NAN -

ALL-PURPOSE WHOLE WHEAT BAKING MIX

Q I enjoy camping with my family. Do you or any of your readers know of a recipe for an all-purpose whole wheat baking mix that I could use for biscuits, muffins, and pancakes? It would sure make cooking easier away from home.

CAROLYN
Windsor, Vermont

A Here's a recipe for an all-purpose baking mix that you can store in an airtight container in your fridge or freezer for up to eight months.

9 cups whole wheat pastry flour
1½ cups instant powdered milk
3 tablespoons baking powder
2 teaspoons cream of tartar
1 teaspoon baking soda
1½ cups cold butter

Combine all ingredients, except butter, in a large bowl. Cut in butter until evenly distributed and the pieces are the size of small peas.

BISCUITS

2 cups of the mix
½ cup water

Bake in a 425-degree preheated oven for about 10–12 minutes.

MUFFINS

2½ cups mix
¾ cup cold water
1 egg
2 tablespoons honey

Preheat oven to 400 degrees and mix water, egg, and honey. Stir in the baking mix until it's barely moistened and nearly fill greased muffin tins almost to the top. Bake about 20 minutes or until brown.

PANCAKES

4 cups mix
2 eggs
3 cups water

Beat water and eggs and then add the mix. Cook the cakes on a lightly greased preheated griddle.

A GOAT BUTTER CORRESPONDENCE

Q You never did say if goat butter is made in Vermont or not.

E.A.W.
Rutland, Vermont
January 10, 1988

A As to goat butter, sorry we didn't reply sooner. It is not made in Vermont. There are a number of reasons for this, but the main one is that there just isn't enough available goat's milk to meet the already existing demand, and it's more profitable for goat dairy farmers to sell their raw milk to cheese-making or to milk-processing plants. Also, making butter from goat's milk is a complicated process; goat's milk is naturally homogenized, and, unlike cow's milk, doesn't separate out by itself. Finally, to sell goat butter over the counter, it would have to be made from pasteurized milk, and the pasteurization equipment is too expensive for the small goat dairy farmer.

Q I know you haven't forgotten it. Nor can I forget it every time the hecklers see me and ask if I like goat's butter. I had asked you if (government) surplus butter was made in Vermont. Your reply was on how GOAT'S BUTTER was made. I have been the GOAT ever since and still do not know if GOV'T (GOVERNMENT) SURPLUS BUTTER IS MADE HERE. Have a great day.

> E.A.W. ("GOAT")
> Rutland, Vermont
> October 9, 1989

A Thank you for a good morning laugh! Sorry to have misread your letter, but—at the risk of being boring—your misadventure was a good example of what happens when people don't write legibly. We are sometimes unable to answer letters at all because we can't manage to decipher them. Now in answer to your extremely legible second request for information: Saint Albans Cooperative

Creamery used to sell surplus butter to the federal government. They made nonfat dry milk, and there was a lot of cream left over, which they then made into butter. However, it has been ten years or more since they have had any extra to sell. Ben & Jerry's, Howard Johnson's, and Brigham's Ice Cream buy up all the surplus they have left ... no surplus cream equals no surplus butter.

About six months later we received yet another letter from E.A.W., who had apparently missed our reply in the paper.

Q How much longer are you going to leave me in the GOAT skin? About two years ago, I wrote and asked you about GOVERNMENT SURPLUS BUTTER. Your reply was details on how to make GOAT'S BUTTER. GOVT is the abbreviation for *Government*. How can you get GOAT out of GOVT and there was no S on GOVT. I still would like to know where government surplus butter is made. It is of outstanding quality. Why isn't store butter of the same quality? Required to meet the same standards. Then the customer would get a pound of butter that could be called butter!

E.A.W.
Mendon, Vermont
February 4, 1990

A You old goat, we apologize for leaving you stuck in a goatskin. In our defense, we had a hard time reading your writing all those years ago; we're sorry to have gotten your goat. And finally, thanks to the University of Vermont Extension Service, we have an answer for you. Government surplus butter is produced the same way as the butter you buy in a grocery store. The same standards are required for commercial and government surplus butter. Most of the government butter is produced in the Midwest and California. Perhaps because it's not produced in New England, it tastes different.

HULLED CORN

Some years ago we published a letter from W. F. of Rutland, Vermont, who was looking for hulled corn for her father to "put in pea soup and eat as is." We included the letter in our first book and received this feedback from M. H. of Randolph Center, Vermont. "Here is a recipe for hulled corn (new way, versus the old lye method) which I copied before being married in 1946.

"Pick over 1 quart dried yellow corn. Cover with 2 quarts water and 2 tablespoons baking soda. Soak overnight. Boil in the same water till hulls are loosened, about three hours, adding more water as needed. Drain, wash, and rub off hulls with hands. Boil corn again in clear water. Change water, add 1 teaspoon salt and boil gently till corn is tender, 4 hours. Serve hot with milk or butter, instead of potatoes. May be warmed up. Yield: 4 quarts."

BEAVER BAY ICE TEA

½ cup orange pekoe tea
1 cup sugar
3 quarts water, use 1½ cups to make the sugar syrup
juice of five lemons
4 large or 5 small sprigs of mint

Boil the remaining 1½ cups of water and pour over the tea. Let stand three minutes; strain; add sugar syrup and mint. Cool and add lemon juice. This will keep three days in the fridge.

RASPBERRY VINEGAR

Q I've seen several recipes that call for raspberry vinegar. I have a huge raspberry patch and would like to make some vinegar. How do I do it?

A REGULAR READER
Rutland, Vermont

A 2 cups white vinegar (5 percent acidity)
1 pint fresh raspberries
1 cup sugar

Combine vinegar and raspberries in a 1-quart glass jar; bruise the berries with a wooden spoon to release juice. Let stand in a cool, dark place for two weeks. Strain juice into a medium saucepan and add sugar. Stirring constantly, bring to a boil and then boil gently for 2 minutes. Cool; skim and place in a clean bottle or jar. Store in a refrigerator. Makes about 2½ cups.

JIM BATES'S YUMMY BARBECUED BEANS

1 teaspoon ground oregano
1 teaspoon cumin
6 teaspoons coarse black pepper
3 teaspoons minced dried onion
6 teaspoons ground marjoram
5 bay leaves
1 teaspoon coarse ground red pepper
6 teaspoons Chili Quick or other instant chili mix
1 teaspoon chili powder
2 teaspoons garlic salt
1 cup barbecue sauce
pinto beans
onions, chopped
pork or bacon ends, optional

Mix all of the above. For each pound of beans you are going to cook, use ¼ cup of this mixture. Put the balance in plastic bags or a jar and store in the freezer. Soak pinto beans overnight, and in the morning rinse once. Fry up ¼ pound of salt pork or bacon ends and one large chopped onion for each pound of beans. Cook the beans in plenty of water, and when the water starts to boil, add the onions, pork or bacon ends, and the spice mixture, but *only after the water starts to boil*. Once the beans come to a boil, cut the fire down until they just simmer (bubbles must show, but that's all). After the beans have cooked for 2½ or 3 hours, add 1 cup of barbecue sauce, and continue to cook for ½ hour more. One pound of beans serves eight generously.

WHIPPED DRY MILK

Q Do you or any of your readers have the recipe for whipping "dry milk"? I have lost mine. It was the same texture as whipped cream.

B.B.
Chester, Vermont

A Chill beaters and in a narrow, deep bowl stir together ¼ cup dry milk with ¼ cup ice water. Beat on the highest speed until peaks form. For a tasty topping, you can add iced orange or pineapple juice in place of the water. To make the topping even tastier, when you have whipped the milk, add 1 teaspoon lemon juice, beat again until stiff, then blend in 2 tablespoons frozen unsweetened apple juice concentrate. Yield: 1¾ cups; 6 calories per serving.

DEAR ANNE AND NAN -

Reseasoning Waffle Irons

If your waffles stick, reseason your waffle iron by first removing all the old bits of waffle from the iron (a toothbrush helps). Heat up the waffle iron to medium and brush vegetable oil across the top and bottom griddle. Give it a quick and careful swipe with a paper towel to wipe up the excess. Do this for the first couple of batches. We've found that adding a bit more shortening to the recipe also helps the sticking problem.

MAPLE OATMEAL BREAD

Q While at the Champlain Valley Fair, I bought some maple bread at the Maple Sugar House. Could you please find the recipe for this delicious bread?

M.B.S.
Barre, Vermont

A This is the best maple bread there is. We hope it's the one you're looking for.

¾ cup boiling water
1 cup hot coffee
1 cup rolled oats

⅓ cup shortening
½ cup maple syrup
5½ cups sifted bread flour or enough to make stiff dough
½ cup sugar
2 teaspoons salt
2 packages dry yeast
¼ cup lukewarm water
2 eggs, unbeaten

Combine boiling water, coffee, rolled oats, shortening, maple syrup, sugar, and salt. Let this mixture cool until lukewarm. Dissolve yeast in ¼ cup lukewarm water and add to the first mixture. Blend in the eggs. Gradually add the sifted flour and mix until smooth. Add enough more flour to make a stiff dough. Place in a greased bowl, cover, and let rise until double in size. Knead a very little and divide into two loaves. Place in two well-greased bread pans. Let rise again and bake in moderate oven, 350 degrees, for 1 hour.

BEER BREAD

E.A.P. of Rutland, Vermont wrote asking for a recipe for beer bread. We received ninety-four responses and sixty-eight of them were for the same recipe. Here it is.

3 cups self-rising flour

3 tablespoons white sugar

1 12-ounce can of beer (about half of you say the beer should be room temperature, and many said not to use light beer).

Mix together thoroughly. Pour into greased bread pan and bake at 375 degrees for 45 minutes.

Variations on the above:

BEER BREAD À LA BILL
from E.E. of Worcester, Vermont

Eliminate the sugar and melt 7 tablespoons of sweet butter. Pour 4 tablespoons of sweet butter over the bread before you put it in the oven. Bake for 20 minutes and then pour on the remaining butter and bake for 20 minutes more.

QUICK RAISIN CINNAMON BEER BREAD

2 cups unsifted self-rising flour

1 cup whole wheat flour

1½ teaspoons baking powder

1 teaspoon cinnamon

½ teaspoon nutmeg

¼ teaspoon cloves

1 12-ounce can beer
1 tablespoon honey or 3 tablespoons sugar
1 cup raisins

Grease a 9″ × 5″ loaf pan. Combine flours, baking powder, and spices in a large bowl, stirring together until well mixed. Add beer, honey or sugar, and the raisins. Mix until well blended. Pour batter into prepared pan. Bake in preheated 350-degree oven for 45 minutes or until wooden toothpick inserted in the middle comes out clean. Turn out on a rack to cool.

DARK RYE BEER BREAD

from the Sunrise Bakery in Brandon, Vermont

1 cup warm water or milk
3 cups beer at room temperature
½ cup molasses
½ cup brown sugar
¼ cup melted butter
2 eggs
3 envelopes dry yeast
1 tablespoon salt
1 tablespoon caraway seed
5 cups medium rye flour

In a large mixing bowl, mix milk or water, beer, molasses, and sugar; stir in yeast to dissolve. Let sit about 10 minutes. Add salt, butter, eggs to the mixture. Stir in flours and caraway seeds to make a soft but stiff dough. Put dough on a floured board and knead for 5–6 minutes. Cover and let rise until doubled. Cut dough in half and shape into loaves. Let rise until doubled. Bake in 350-degree oven 50–60 minutes.

LITE BREAD

Q I like the idea of the new "lite" breads now sold in supermarkets, but I prefer to bake my own. Do you or does anyone have a bread recipe for "lite" bread, especially whole wheat?

P.H.N.
Weston, Vermont

A Our food expert, Pat Baril, told us that most of the calories in bread come from the starch in the flour. Many diet breads are made with gluten, a high-protein whole wheat flour from which the starch has been removed. Natural food stores carry gluten flour.

10–11 cups whole wheat gluten flour
3 packages active dry yeast
2 teaspoons salt
½ cup honey
⅓ cup cold butter or margarine

5 cups very warm water (120–130 degrees)
2 cups wheat germ
melted shortening

Mix together half of the flour (5 cups) with yeast and salt in a large bowl. Add honey, butter, and water; mix until a thick, elastic batter is formed. Gradually beat in as much of the remaining flour and wheat germ as possible. Add remainder by kneading 8–10 minutes. Place dough in a large greased bowl; cover and let rise in a warm place until doubled in bulk, about 1½ hours. Punch dough down; divide into three equal portions, and allow dough to rest for 10 minutes. Shape into loaves and place in greased bread tins; brush top with melted shortening. Cover loaves with a light cloth and let rise in a warm place until double in bulk, about 1 hour. Bake in a preheated 375-degree oven 40–45 minutes.

Self-rising Flour

For those of us who don't have any self-rising flour in the pantry, J.R. of Rutland, Vermont tells us how to make it.

Combine:
8 cups all-purpose flour
5 tablespoons baking powder
2 tablespoons sugar
1 tablespoon salt

Sift three times, store in a well-sealed plastic bag.

Rubber Jar Rings for Canning

We searched for these, and so did many of our readers. The Ball Company stopped making them because they and the U.S. Department of Agriculture "no longer recommend closures that seal with jar rubbers for home canning. These closures have a higher incidence of failure than two-piece dome lids. Old jars requiring jar rubbers for sealing are also more susceptible to breakage." A vigilant reader sent us a copy of an article from the 1990 *Herald Grange* that said, in part, "The U.S.D.A. had not passed a ruling that would prohibit the manufacture and sale of glass canning jar rubbers.... Times do change and so do manufacturers' products." If you want rubber jar rings, we've found a source but there's a hitch. They are only available by the case. Don't despair; find a friend or a merchant to share a case, as some of our readers did. The company is Allied Plastics, 925 Orchard Lake Road, Pontiac, MI 48053.

TRIPE

Q I am looking for a way to fry tripe to make it brown.

D.L.
Corinth, Vermont

A Cut into square pieces and lay it on a paper towel or a hand towel to get all the moisture out. Make a batter with:

1 cup flour
¼ teaspoon salt
½ cup cold water
1 egg, well beaten
½ tablespoon vinegar
1 teaspoon olive oil or melted butter

Mix salt and flour. Add water gradually. When smooth, add egg, vinegar, and oil. Dip tripe in batter. Have fat hot and fry. As the tripe gets brown turn over and brown other side. Then turn heat down and cook about an hour. This batter serves about 1½ pounds. If not cooked through, turn heat up at the last minute and brown until crisp.

Frozen Fish

If you buy your frozen fish in 5-pound lots and only want to eat a little at a time, put the package in your fridge. In 24 hours you'll be able to separate the fish into the size portions that you want. As long as there are still crystals in the center of the fish, it's fine to refreeze it.

RAG MUFFINS

▷◁

Q A restaurant in Enosburg Falls has on its menu "Rag Muffins." Can you get the recipe, please?

E.G.
Reading, Vermont

A Without the name of the restaurant we were stumped, but our dear readers sent us several recipes for rag muffins.

RAG MUFFINS I
from I.H. of Rutland, Vermont

Make baking-powder biscuit dough. Roll out as for pie crust. Spread with margarine, brown sugar, or hard maple sugar and sprinkle with cinnamon. Roll up as for jelly roll. Slice into individual biscuits and bake in a greased baking pan in a moderate oven (350 degrees) until nice and brown on top.

RAG MUFFINS II
from A.H. of Manchester Center, Vermont

Put some maple syrup in a lightly greased glass pie plate and use refrigerated biscuits from the supermarket. To be sure they cook on the bottom, put them on a lower rack in oven. Bake at about 375 degrees. Cool briefly, and when you remove the biscuit from the pan, be sure to wipe up some of the maple syrup.

DOUGHNUTS WITHOUT MILK, *thanks to J.W. of North Clarendon, Vermont*

2 cups sugar
6 eggs
16 ounces sour cream
2 teaspoons nutmeg
¼ teaspoon ginger
1 teaspoon baking soda

Beat all the ingredients together and add 7 cups of flour. Let sit for 24 hours. Then cut and fry.

Perfect Doughnuts

To keep your doughnuts from cracking open or the holes closing up, keep the temperature of the fat in which you're frying them at 365 degrees. The best way to make a perfect doughnut is in a thermostatically controlled electric fry pan. The next-best way is to use a fat thermometer, taking the temperature of the fat between each batch. If you don't have a fat thermometer, you can measure the approximate temperature of the fat by throwing in a bread cube and counting to 60. If by the end of your count the bread cube has turned golden brown, your fat is ready.

PICKLES

ᗢᗢᗢᗢᗢᗢᗢᗢᗢᗢᗢᗢᗢᗢᗢᗢᗢᗢᗢᗢᗢᗢᗢᗢᗢᗢᗢᗢᗢᗢᗢᗢᗢᗢᗢᗢᗢᗢᗢ

Q Third request! Can you give me a recipe for sour pickles?

S.G.
Montpelier, Vermont

A Whew! Thank you for being so patient and persistent! B.D. sent us a recipe this week. He writes, "I have a recipe for sour pickles that A.L. gave me back in August of 1977. He canned a lot. These are sour pickles and I mean sour. I love them."

SOUR PICKLES

1 cup sugar
1 cup salt
1 cup dry mustard
2½ quarts regular vinegar
1½ quarts water
1 teaspoon alum (for crispness)
½ teaspoon whole pickling spices to each quart

"This solution will make about 12 quarts of pickles. Fill your jars with small or cut-up large cucumbers, put in the ½ teaspoon of whole pickling spices, and fill with the solution. Ready to eat in about a month but better if left longer. You may have to stir the solution once in a while because the mustard comes to the top." F.C. of Springfield, Vermont, also sent us a recipe and noted, "Let pickles cure a month or longer before eating, depending on how much you like to pucker. These go good with hot maple syrup and a homemade doughnut."

FROZEN ZUCCHINI OR CUCUMBER PICKLES

J.F. came to our rescue with this recipe that was given to her by her uncle, F.J., who had these pickles at a seniors'-meal site in Burlington, Vermont.

Peel and slice two quarts of cukes or zukes. Add one large onion and 1½ tablespoons salt. Let sit for three hours. Pour off and rinse the zukes or cukes. Make a sauce of 1 cup vinegar, 1½ cups sugar, ½ teaspoon alum. Pour over zukes and freeze.

ZUCCHINI BREAD-AND-BUTTER PICKLES

1 quart distilled white vinegar
2 cups sugar
3 tablespoons salt
2 teaspoons celery seed
2 teaspoons turmeric or dill seed
1 teaspoon dry mustard
4 quarts sliced zucchini
1 quart sliced onions

Bring vinegar, sugar, salt, and spices to a boil. Pour over freshly sliced vegetables. Let stand for 1 hour. Bring to a boil and cook for 3 minutes. Pack into hot, sterilized jars. Seal. Process for 10 minutes. Makes 6 to 7 pints.

DILLY BEANS

Q Please can you find me a recipe for dill-pickled green beans. I had some at a bean supper and want to make some.

R.O.C.
Roxbury, Vermont

A Here is our favorite Dilly Bean recipe.

4 pounds green beans
6 tablespoons salt
3 cups distilled white vinegar
3 cups water
1 tablespoon dill seed or fresh dill
1 tablespoon mustard seed
18 whole black peppercorns or 1½ teaspoons dried hot red peppers, seeds removed and pepper crushed

Wash beans thoroughly and cut in small pieces, or use whole small beans. Combine salt, vinegar, and water. Heat to boiling. Pack beans into hot, sterilized jars. Add to each jar ½ teaspoon dill seed or fresh dill head, ½ teaspoon mustard seed, and 3 whole peppercorns or ¼ teaspoon hot red peppers. Process in boiling water for 20 minutes. Makes 6 to 7 pints.

DEBBIE BRUSH'S SUMMER COOLER

Take 4 cups of fresh rhubarb and cook until soft. Add 4 cups of strawberries and ½ cup of sugar. Cook until the sugar is dissolved and the fruit is mushy. Put the fruit into a sieve that has been placed over a bowl so the juice can drip through. When the juice has dripped through, store it in a jar. Add about ¼ cup to a glass of soda water or ginger ale for a refreshing summertime beverage. The stewed fruit is good alone and especially delicious on ice cream.

Cooking with Alcohol

If a recipe calls for alcohol and you're concerned about the alcoholic content, say rum in a cake, don't worry. The alcohol evaporates when you cook it at a high temperature, only the taste remains.

Black Pepper Versus White Pepper

The difference between black and white pepper is the time they are picked. Both are the fruit of the *piper nigrum* plant, native to Asia. Black pepper is picked while the berry is unripe and is dried until it becomes wrinkled, shriveled, and black. It has more bite than white pepper, which is simply the mature berry with its outer coating removed. White pepper, being more labor-intensive, is more expensive than the black and is considered by some to be a superior product.

CHOCOLATE CRINKLE PUFF COOKIES

Many readers came to P.W.'s aid when she lost the recipe for these.

½ cup vegetable oil
4 squares unsweetened chocolate
2 cups sugar
4 eggs
2 teaspoons vanilla
2 cups flour
½ teaspoon salt

2 teaspoons baking powder
½ cup confectioner's sugar

Mix oil, chocolate, and sugar. Blend in vanilla and one egg at a time; add flour, baking powder, and salt. Chill several hours or overnight. Roll into balls, roll in confectioner's sugar, and place on greased cookie sheet 2 inches apart. Bake 10–12 minutes. Do not overbake. Makes about 6 dozen cookies.

ALMOND MACAROON COOKIES

Q I have been searching for ages for a really great almond macaroon. A cookie that is crisp on the outside and soft, plump, and moist on the inside. I don't want to use store-bought almond paste. I prefer to start from scratch using my own ground almonds.

D.S.
Proctorsville, Vermont

A 8 egg whites
1 pound (2¼ cups) granulated sugar
1 pound almonds, fine-ground in food processor or blender
1 teaspoon vanilla

Beat egg whites until foamy. Add sugar, 2 tablespoons at a time, and beat for 30 minutes, then add vanilla and ground nuts. Refrigerate for several hours, then drop by teaspoonfuls onto cookie sheets lined with unglazed paper. Let stand overnight. Bake in preheated 300-degree oven for about 1 hour or until cookies can be lifted from the paper. Makes 7 dozen.

CHOCOLATE DREAM DESSERT

Q My mom used to make a dessert using cooked chocolate pudding and, I believe, cream cheese. It's possible she got it from one of the Kraft recipes on television in the 1960s. She passed away suddenly fourteen years ago and was the only person I knew who made this dessert.

R.L.
Rutland, Vermont

A P.P. kindly sent this along and said it is very popular at potluck dinners.

Combine ½ cup margarine, 1 cup flour, 1 tablespoon sugar, and ½ cup chopped nuts. Press into a 9″ × 13″ pan. Bake 10 minutes and allow to cool.

Beat together 8 ounces cream cheese and 1 cup confectioner's sugar and add one large container of thawed Cool Whip and mix thoroughly. Spread on cooled crust. Mix two packages instant chocolate pudding with 3 cups milk and spread over cream layer. Refrigerate. The dessert can be decorated with chopped nuts, sprinkles, etc.

Devil's Food Cake

The difference between chocolate cake and devil's food cake is that devil's food cake is lighter in texture than regular chocolate cake and is so named because of its color contrast to angel food cake, its white fluffy counterpart.

NEEDHAM CANDY

Q I used to buy these candies made with mashed potatoes in Portland, Maine. I've lost the recipe; does anyone know how to make them?

L.J.
Montpelier, Vermont

A ¾ cup mashed potato
½ teaspoon salt
2 1-pound packages confectioner's sugar

1 stick margarine
½ pound flaked coconut
2 teaspoons vanilla

Pare and cook potato to make ¾ cup mashed potato, not seasoned. Add salt. Using a double boiler, place the stick of margarine in it and melt over boiling water. Add mashed potato, confectioner's sugar, flaked coconut, and vanilla. Mix well, then turn into a buttered jelly roll pan. Spread evenly. Place in a cool place to harden. When hard, cut into small squares and dip in the following chocolate mixture.

CHOCOLATE DIP

1 12-ounce package of chocolate bits
4 squares unsweetened chocolate
½ cake paraffin (2½″ × 2½″, yes, the same paraffin you melt to use on top of jelly)

Use double boiler again. Place paraffin in top over boiling water to melt. Then add the two kinds of chocolate. Allow chocolate to melt. Stir well to mix ingredients. A toothpick or cake tester may be used to dip the Needham squares. Hold each square above the chocolate mixture after dipping, so that the square drains well. Place on waxed paper to harden. Recipe will make 66 good-sized Needhams.

NEW YORK ICE CREAM

ᗝᗝ

Q Years ago, when I was a child, my mother used to make a homemade ice cream called New York Ice Cream. She made some type of custard, put it in ice cube trays, and after it was partially frozen, she would [stir it and] put it back in the trays. It was the most delicious, creamiest ice cream I have ever had. When I asked for the recipe, she said that she was sure she had discarded the cookbook years ago. Do any of your readers recall this treat? I sure would love the recipe, cholesterol or not!

L.D.
Manchester Center, Vermont

A 1¼ cups of top milk or light cream
2 eggs, separated
½ cup sugar
1 tablespoon flour
1 cup whipping cream or evaporated milk
2 teaspoons vanilla
salt

Scald milk or light cream. Beat egg yolks, adding sugar and flour. Combine with hot milk or light cream and cook on low heat until mixture coats a spoon, like a custard. Cool. Beat egg whites until stiff. Add salt and fold into custard; add vanilla. Pour into tray and freeze to mush. Remove from freezer and fold in whipped cream or evaporated milk and freeze.

MARY MERCHANT'S MINT SAUCE

Makes almost 1 pint:

3 cups sugar
1½ cups vinegar
1½ cups water
1 cup mint leaves, chopped fine

Boil sugar, vinegar, and water together until they're the consistency of maple syrup. Add mint leaves and a little green food coloring. Pour into a sterile jar to store.

PRISCILLA'S PERFECT PIECRUST

Q I have a terrible time making piecrust. Often I have to roll it out several times and it ends up tough as leather. Do you have a foolproof recipe?

SUZZ
West Windsor, Vermont

A You can roll this out as many times as you want.

3 cups sifted flour
1 teaspoon salt
1¼ cups Crisco shortening
1 egg
1 tablespoon white vinegar
5 tablespoons water

Cut the shortening into the flour and add the salt. In a separate bowl, mix the egg, 1 tablespoon white vinegar, and 5 tablespoons water. Make a well in the flour mixture and dump the egg mixture into it. Stir and roll. Makes a double crust.

FRIENDSHIP FRUIT

Q Several years ago I had a jar of "Friendship Fruit" given to me. I believe every two weeks I would add fruit and a cup of sugar. When I had over 3 cups, I would divide it and give half to a friend who would continue adding fruit and sugar every two weeks. I would like to make this again. However, I don't have the instructions on how to start the fruit mixture.

MARCIE
Rutland, Vermont

A We received three basic variations for making the fruit from our readers. One that uses brandy in the starter, one using yeast, and the third using no yeast and no alcohol.

STARTER WITH YEAST
from C.R., Wallingford, Vermont

¾ cup drained canned peaches, cut into pieces
¾ cup drained pineapple chunks
1½ cups sugar
6 maraschino cherries
1 package (¼ ounce) instant dry yeast

Combine the above and place in a jar with a loose cover—an apothecary jar is perfect. Stir several times the first day, then stir once a day. At the end of two weeks the starter has fermented enough to make the sauce.

STARTER WITH BRANDY
from M.B., Rutland, Vermont

1 cup cling peaches, drained and cut into small pieces
1 cup sugar
1 cup brandy (apricot is great)

Mix above ingredients using a wooden spoon or rubber spatula (*no metal!*). Place in a crock or a glass jar with a loose cover. Allow to sit on shelf two weeks before stirring. *Do not refrigerate.* Keep jar in a warm place, like next to your stove.

FRIENDSHIP FRUIT WITH NO STARTER
from E.C.R., Barre, Vermont

1 cup pineapple chunks, drained
1 cup sugar

Let stand for two weeks and then add:

1 cup sliced peaches
1 cup sugar

Let stand for two weeks and then add:

1 cup maraschino cherries, drained
1 cup sugar

Let stand for two weeks, then repeat the entire procedure. Never refrigerate.

FRIENDSHIP FRUIT WITH STARTER

½ cup starter
1 jar (8 ounces) maraschino cherries
1 1-pound can pineapple
1 can peaches

Drain fruit, cut cherries in half, cut pineapple and peaches into equally small pieces. Mix all together using wooden spoon. Place in a glass jar with loose lid. Store in a warm place. Stir once or twice a week. Never refrigerate unless you want to stop the fermenting.

To keep active: Once every two weeks, add 1 cup cherries or 1 cup pineapple or 1 cup peaches and 1 cup sugar. Never let the contents get below the 3-cup level or the fermentation will stop. Takes about four weeks before it's ready to eat. Original starter can be passed on in ½-cup portions. Whenever you have more than 3 cups of fruit, you may divide it into two portions and give it to a friend.

THE WORLD'S BEST FUDGE SAUCE

1 tablespoon butter
1 square chocolate
⅓ cup boiling water
1 cup sugar
2 tablespoons white Karo syrup
½ teaspoon vanilla

Melt butter and chocolate over very low heat. Add boiling water slowly, stirring constantly. Add sugar and syrup and stir until dissolved. Simmer 4–5 minutes. Cool slightly and add vanilla. Serve hot or cold.

WINE MAKING

⌁⌁⌁

Q I know that wine is made from grapes! But how do you do it? Do you need a kit? I have a beautiful grapevine in my yard that yields big, nice purple grapes every fall. I've looked and looked for some information or recipes and I can't find a thing. I really would like to make my own wine. Would you please help me by finding out what I need and how?

B.F.
Pittsford, Vermont

A Before you go investing in any wine-making equipment, we suggest that you make a "taste test" of the wine you are going to get from your grapes: Mani-schewitz Concord Grape Wine, which is available in your local supermarket, is pretty close to it—heavy and sweet. If you still want to go ahead, Beer and Wine Hobby, P.O. Box M, Melrose, MA 02176 (617-665-8442), will be delighted to send you a free catalogue for everything you will need. Two essentials are a hydrometer and an acid-testing kit. Each sells for about $5. The catalogue also has how-to books of every description. If you should decide that you want to make wine, but don't want to make it from the Concord grapes in your backyard, you can order a wide variety of fresh California vineyard grapes from Beer and Wine Hobby in August and create your own estate-bottled burgundy or chardonnay or whatever!

Cracking Butternuts

A couple of years ago, we had a voluminous correspondence with our readers as to the best way to crack open butternuts. Suggestions ranged from backing over them with a bulldozer to bashing them with a stone and everything in between. However, the greatest number of letters suggested the following: After steaming the nuts for about 20 minutes, put them in a household vise so that either end, rather than either side, touches the vise surfaces. Slowly turn the vise handle until the nut cracks neatly in half, then pick out the perfect, whole nut meat.

DIXIE DELIGHTS FOR OUR LONG WINTER NIGHTS

3 cups peanut butter
⅓ cup butter or margarine
¾ cup dry milk
2¼ cups confectioner's sugar
1 cup chocolate chips
3 tablespoons butter

Stir butter and peanut butter over low heat until mixture is quite thin. Add dry milk and mix well. Sift and mix in confectioner's sugar. Spread in greased

9″ × 13″ pan. Cool in refrigerator for 30–40 minutes or until firm. Melt chocolate chips and butter in a double boiler over hot water. Spread over peanut butter mixture. Allow to cool and cut into squares.

POPCORN BALLS

▽▽

Q Can you or someone in your vast group of readers supply me with instructions for making old-fashioned popcorn balls? I used to make them a long time ago, and now I can't remember how.

B.M.C.

A This is our favorite recipe for popcorn balls. Prepare 3 quarts popcorn and cook the following ingredients to 270 degrees (hard-crack stage).

1 cup molasses
1 cup corn syrup
1 teaspoon vinegar

Stir in 3 tablespoons butter and ⅓ teaspoon salt. Pour slowly over the popcorn and stir with a wooden spoon to coat each kernel. Butter your hands slightly and shape the corn lightly into 3-inch balls. Set on wax paper to harden. After they do, wrap them in wax paper.

SISTER MABEL'S CARAMEL CORN

2 cups firmly packed light brown sugar
½ cup light corn syrup
½ pound margarine or butter
¼ teaspoon cream of tartar
1 teaspoon salt
1 teaspoon baking soda
6 quarts popped corn

In a 2½-quart saucepan, combine brown sugar, corn syrup, margarine or butter, cream of tartar, and salt. Bring to boil, stirring over medium-high heat. Stirring constantly (*very important*), boil rapidly about 5 minutes until mixture reaches 260 degrees (hard ball) on a candy thermometer. Remove from heat. Stir in baking soda quickly but thoroughly. Pour at once over popped corn in large roasting or baking pan. Stir gently until all kernels are coated. Bake at 200 degrees for 1 hour, stirring a couple of times during baking. Turn out at once on wax paper. Spread apart and allow clusters to cool completely. Break into small clusters and store in tightly covered containers. Makes 8 quarts of the best treat imaginable.

Bigger Popcorn

Inexpensive popping corn pops bigger if it's stored in the freezer.

M&M's COOKIES

Q I am looking for a certain M&M's cookie recipe. All I remember of the ingredients are egg whites, sugar, and M&M's. They are a white cookie and, after baking them, they are almost hollow.

J.M.G.
Montpelier, Vermont

A 3 egg whites
¼ teaspoon cream of tartar
⅛ teaspoon salt
½ cup sugar
1 teaspoon vanilla
1 (12-ounce) package semisweet chocolate chips or M&M's

Preheat oven to 200 degrees. Line two large cookie sheets with foil. In a small bowl beat egg whites, cream of tartar, and salt until soft peaks form. Beating at a high speed, gradually beat in sugar, 2 tablespoons at a time. Beat well after each addition until sugar is completely dissolved. Add vanilla and continue beating at high speed until meringue stands in stiff and glossy peaks. Fold in chocolate chips or M&M's. Drop teaspoonfuls 1 inch apart onto foil-covered cookie sheets. Bake 1 hour and 15 minutes or until set. Cool on cookie sheets on wire racks for 10 minutes.

CRYSTALS IN GRAPE JELLY

Q I make wild-grape jelly each year I find grapes. I use only sugar, no pectin. Vermont grapes are so strong, I often use half apple juice. Once in a while I get crystals. I used to know what they were, and I read long ago what I could add to prevent crystallization. I throw away crystallized jars. Does anyone know what to add? I've checked all my cookbooks and with a dietitian.

E.M.
Poultney, Vermont

A Tartaric acid, which is used to make cream of tartar, is found in the juice of grapes, and the crystals in your jelly are tartaric crystals. These crystals won't hurt you, and Alice Wright of the University of Vermont Extension Service knew of nothing you could add to your jelly to prevent them from forming. She did tell us that in *Putting Food By*, author Janet Green suggests holding the grape juice overnight in a cool place and straining again to remove the crystals before making jelly.

KAHLUA—MAKING YOUR OWN

4 cups sugar
4 cups water

2 ounces instant coffee
1 split vanilla bcan
1 fifth 100-proof vodka

Boil sugar and water for syrup. Add coffee and split vanilla bean. Leave 10 minutes, add vodka. Mix and pour into bottles. Makes a bit more than half a gallon.

BRAN BREAD

Q I am looking for a bran recipe that my mother made in the 1920s and 1930s. I remember it contained yeast, Kellogg's All-Bran, flour, molasses, and water.

S.N.
Londonderry, Vermont

A A.G. of Shoreham, Vermont, sent us her mother's recipe for bran bread:

1½ cups boiling water
2 teaspoons salt
⅓ cup butter
⅓ cup brown sugar
2 tablespoons molasses
1 cup warm water

2½ to 3 cups All-Bran or Bran Flakes
5–6 cups flour
2 cakes yeast

Combine boiling water with salt, butter, brown sugar, and molasses in a large bowl. Cool until warm. Dissolve yeast in warm water with a pinch or two of sugar. Stir yeast and bran into hot (now warm) water mix. Stir in half of the flour and beat until smooth. Add more flour to make medium-stiff dough. Place in buttered bowl, cover, and let rise to double in bulk. Turn out on floured board, divide in two parts. Shape into loaves, place in two buttered pans. Cover, let rise to double, then bake at 325 degrees for 1 hour or until done. Brush with melted butter.

HARD CIDER

To make hard cider, put cider in an open container (glass or ceramic) and let sit at about 60 degrees, depending on hardness desired, for up to 10 days. "Rack off" (i.e., pour off) clear cider, leaving all sediment in the bottom. Bottle and cork and put in a cool, dark place for six months or so. For quick hard cider nature's way: after letting ferment for the requisite number of days inside, put container outdoors, let freeze, then pour off clear unfrozen liquid at the top. This "ambrosialike" liquor has too much alcohol content to solidify!

IS IT SAFE? ANSWERS FOR THE COOK

COOKWARE

ALUMINUM

Q What is the health hazard of old 1940–50 aluminum pots? Are they a hazard? If so, why?

> E.B.
> Poultney, Vermont

A A few years ago, researchers discovered that there was a higher than normal concentration of aluminum in the brains of Alzheimer's patients. Dr. Daniel Perl at the University of Vermont was a pioneer in researching the aluminum/Alzheimer's connection. We called him, as one of our readers was concerned about the use of deodorants containing aluminum zirconium. Dr. Perl assured us that his and others' research had shown that there is no evidence that the use of antacids, aluminum cookware, or deodorants (all sources of aluminum) cause or contribute to the disease.

Q At the cottage, we bake beans in a hole in the ground, a pit lined with stones in which a fire burns for several hours. The pot of beans is lowered into the pit and covered with earth, at least for overnight. The heat of the stones and coals bakes the beans. Up to now we have been using a cast-iron kettle, but its capacity is limited. At a recent sale we purchased a large and heavy, ¼-inch-thick aluminum kettle, and we would like to know if it will withstand our pit cooking. We would hate to warp it and destroy it for future use.

G.P.
St. Johnsbury, Vermont

A The fact that your kettle is so thick means that the aluminum has been cast and so should not warp. If it were sheet aluminum, the chances are that it would. As a rule of thumb, incidentally, warping occurs when a cooking utensil goes from a very cold to a very hot surface (or vice versa), or when its contents no longer contain any moisture; neither of which would pertain, we assume, in your case.

Q Bleach was inadvertently put in an aluminum saucepan. The coating has been removed. Is it safe to use the pan?

K.V.
Westminster West, Vermont

A You don't specify what the coating on the pan was, so we'll try to cover all the bases. If the coating was Teflon, it is better not to use the pan, as the Teflon and bleach have reacted together chemically. Any that is left on the surface of the pan will start coming off in flakes, and your food will pick up the material. Incidentally, in researching this question, we learned that in two or three years Teflon will be entirely phased out and replaced by the Silverstone process. Teflon is a painted-on coating that, like any paint, will peel and flake. Silverstone, on the other hand, is applied under high pressure with a high-speed "gun" and impregnates the metal. If scratched or burned or bleached, Silverstone, unlike Teflon, will not be affected. If the "coating" was actually a high-buff finish, and the bleach made it look dull, there is no harm in using the pan; it just doesn't look as pretty.

COPPER

Q I accidentally overheated a copper kettle, and some of the tin lining chipped off. Is it safe to heat water without the lining intact? If not, I would like to know if it's possible to have it relined and who could do it.

J.A.
Groton, Vermont

A It's safe to use but not very good for the kettle. Heat will tend to warp the untinned copper. The Tinning Company, 69 Norman Street, Everett, MA 02149 (617-389-3400), will be able to re-tin it for you.

ENAMEL

▽▽

Q I have a nested set of enameled cooking pans, purchased from an army-navy store fifteen years ago. Now that time and use have rendered lots of chips and dents, some vague warning runs through my head. "Never use a chipped enameled pan for cooking," my mother warned me years ago. When I asked her what would happen, she didn't know. My question to you is: is cooking with a chipped and dented enameled pan dangerous? Beside the obvious things like ingesting enameled chips and eating rust, I can think of no reason for it to be dangerous.

M.G.
Castleton, Vermont

A The porous surface that chips leave could provide a breeding ground for bacteria. Also, although you don't say what metal the pans are made from—aluminum? tin? a combination of both?—you should be aware that certain foods react with certain metals during the cooking process in a way that is not beneficial to one's health. High-acid food, for example, should never be prepared in aluminum pans. We think you should retire your nested pans and use them for something other than preparing the family meals.

GARBAGE-CAN COOKING

Q I am a member of a camper's group who has been enjoying "garbage-can" dinners. To make this meal, contributions of vegetable, meat, or seafood are layered into a 30-gallon galvanized can. Liquid and seasoning are added and the whole thing is simmered over an open fire. Somewhere I heard that this may be toxic. Can you find out for me what the chemical reaction is, if any, and is there a risk in eating food prepared this way?

V.W.
Poultney, Vermont

A While researching an answer to your question, we discovered that "galvanizing" is a process by which tin or steel is coated with zinc. Armed with this knowledge, we spoke with our local Vermont Extension Service home economist, who said she didn't know whether cooking in a galvanized container was toxic or not. She did mention that when drying fruits or vegetables, one should never use galvanized screening, as it's coated with a mixture of zinc and cadmium and the latter is very toxic.

The three doctors we contacted thought cooking in a galvanized container was a terrible idea but had no scientific reason for their opinion. One doc pointed out that maple syrup evaporating pans are sometimes galvanized, but these have been purposely designed to withstand high temperatures, which one presumes garbage cans have not. Zinc is normally present in the body in small quantities, and a great deal of it has to be ingested before a toxic reaction occurs. This reaction takes the form of nausea, diarrhea, vomiting, fever, and chills. It's hard to tell, should these symptoms occur, whether you have food poisoning or zinc poisoning!

The toxic substance, if it's present, would be the cadmium rather than zinc, and the only way to find out if the latter is used in the galvanizing process would be to call the company that manufactures your garbage can. Until you know for sure, we suggest you cook your meals in something else.

FOOD

DECAFFEINATED COFFEE

Q I keep buying "water-processed" decaffeinated coffee for $10 per pound, thinking it has no traces of the chemicals or suspected carcinogens used to make ordinary decaf. I also keep wondering if I'm being wise or being had. Do you have any info on how coffee is "water-processed," are there ways a consumer can verify that it was indeed "water-processed," and what is the latest info on the health hazards of ordinary decaf? I would greatly appreciate your ending my mental chatter each time I approach the coffee section of the supermarket.

R.R.
Rutland, Vermont

A We got on the phone to David Mullen at Green Mountain Coffee Roasters in Waterbury. He told us that the chemical, or indirect solvent, method of decaffeinating coffee uses methylene chloride on the green beans, and so far there have been no conclusive tests showing that the traces that remain after beans have been roasted are in any way harmful. The buzzword here is, of course, "conclusive."

In the "water process" the green beans are soaked in a tank filled with water. The water is then withdrawn into a second tank, where it's passed through an active carbon filtration system, and then returned to the first tank and reabsorbed into the green beans. There is no way you can tell if the coffee you buy for $10 a pound (which seems awfully expensive to us) has been actually "water processed" as claimed, except the person making the claim would be in serious trouble with the Food and Drug Administration if it was false.

DRIED BEANS, RICE, AND PASTA

Q I wonder about the keeping qualities of dried food. How long is it safe to keep dried beans, rice, and pasta? A friend moved and left me boxes of odds and ends from her pantry. Are these dried items sufficiently mummified to last forever?

B.Z.
Woodstock, Vermont

DEAR ANNE AND NAN -

A Dried food doesn't last forever. It's important to store food properly to maximize nutrient retention. This is achieved by storing the food in airtight containers and keeping these in dark cool places. Pastas, dried beans, and grains can be kept for up to thirty-six months.

GRAY HAMBURGER

Q I have just returned from the supermarket for the umpteenth time with a package of hamburger, opened it immediately, and discovered beneath the rosy-red first layer a gray blob of some inedible-looking stuff, presumably a beef product. Is it safe to consume? Can it be safely frozen for use at a later date? And is there no law to protect the consumer from a product that is represented as fresh-ground but has obviously sat around for many days and may even have been previously frozen? Finally, who invented the diabolical machine which so ingeniously compresses this hideous-looking mess inside a paper-thin layer of tempting-looking and truly fresh ground beef?

N.R.
Rutland, Vermont

A We agree with you; the hamburger one buys in the supermarket does look as if it were the result of a widespread hideous conspiracy perpetrated on the unwary consumer. Take heart. Appearances are deceiving, even deceptive appearances.

Let us take your questions one by one.

The hamburger is completely safe; check the date on the package if you have any doubts about how long it has been on the shelf. Packaged meats are automatically dated by law at the same time they are wrapped and priced.

The hamburger can safely be frozen. However, it's a good idea to take the meat out of the package and rewrap it in freezer paper. Ground beef should not be frozen for more than eight months because of its high fat content.

The "diabolical machine" is the one that wraps the hamburger in plastic wrap, which, adhering tightly to the surface of the hamburger, keeps the portion it touches from discoloring by effectively preventing any oxygen from getting to the surface of the meat. All red meat will discolor fairly rapidly when exposed to oxygen.

STORAGE OF POTATOES IN GARAGE

Q Now that we are harvesting our fall crops, storage of them seems to be a problem. Our cellar is too warm, but our garage is the ideal temperature. We built racks in the front and cover them loosely. Will these vegetables absorb any carbon dioxide or other pollutants from the exhaust fumes of the car?

STORAGE DILEMMA
Pittsford, Vermont

A We spoke to the sanitation supervisor at the Vermont Department of Health and he said that if you left your car running in the garage for a long time, the veggies would absorb some pollutants. He didn't think the storage you describe poses any danger.

COTTONSEED OIL

Q Label reading reveals that cottonseed oil is widely used as a vegetable shortening in commercially baked goods—breads, cookies, crackers, etc.—and also a main ingredient in breath mints. I've heard that since cotton is grown primarily as a textile, rather than a food crop, farmers are allowed to control insect pests and weevils with substances that are not allowed on food crops. I would like to know if this is true and, if possible, what chemicals are most commonly sprayed on cotton crops.

P.F.D.
Mendon, Vermont

A Dr. Steve Brown, down at the State of Alabama Extension Service, said that what you read is true: the seed comes from the same cotton used for textiles and is sprayed with pesticides. However, he said, the pesticide content of cottonseed oil is carefully controlled and monitored by the Environmental Protection Agency (EPA) and has without exception been well below the tolerance level set by the EPA. We were unable to find out what types of pesticides are most commonly used, because we couldn't seem to catch up with Ron Smith, the fellow who, according to the Extension Service, knows the answer. Write him at Extension Hall, Department of Entomology, Auburn University, AL 36849. (That isn't a misprint, there is no town name.)

COOKING VEGGIES IN HARD WATER

Q A knowledgeable friend of mine tells me that vegetables should not be cooked in hard water, as it has some sort of undesirable effect on them. Is this indeed the case? If so, why? My water is very hard.

N.C.
Benson, Vermont

A The presence of calcium, iron, and magnesium makes water hard. As far as we can determine, there's nothing wrong with cooking veggies in hard water. The problems with cooking vegetables in hard water fall into two categories: aesthetic and practical. If there are large amounts of magnesium and iron in your water, it will be brownish and may smell. It won't hurt you to cook veggies in this water, it just may not be very appealing. The iron, in fact is good nutritionally, although it may not be absorbed as well as the iron in meat. There are some practical problems that go with cooking in hard water. For instance, if you try to cook kidney beans in water with a high level of calcium, they'll never soften. The beans will have absorbed calcium while they were soaking in the hard water and again while cooking, and they'll be hard to eat.

IMPORTED SHELLFISH

Q Today, as I ate my oyster stew made from a can of oysters (Geisha brand, product of Korea), I wondered what assurances we have that such imported shellfish is wholesome. We buy baby clams and tiny shrimp labeled as products of Malaysia, and eat them all trustingly. Are we being foolhardy? We hear horror stories of pollution in our own water where shellfish are gathered and we are warned against eating clams during "red tides." How can we assume that Asian waters are any less polluted?

B.N.W.
Perkinsville, Vermont

A We spoke to some folks at the Food and Drug Administration who said that imported canned shellfish is spot checked for bacteria counts and that all foreign canning plants must meet USDA food-processing standards. However, the gentleman we spoke with said that, as far as he knew, the only fish or shellfish headed for canneries that is checked for heavy metal or other pollution-related indicators (i.e., PCBs) is tuna.

CHAPTER 9

UNCLASSIFIED
INFORMATION

What are sinuses for? Where does one get baby shoes bronzed? And is there a use for old used stamps? Read on; this chapter is filled with information that can't be classified but includes some of our favorite questions.

WHAT ARE SINUSES FOR?

Q What are sinuses for? No one I've asked seems to know. Do they have a physiological function? Or are they just cavities in my head that get clogged and infected from time to time?

CURIOUS IN THE MORNING
Plainfield, Vermont

A Sinuses have a threefold purpose. First, they act as a resonator for sound. We all know what happens to our voices when they fill up. It's like shouting in a cave stuffed with cotton. Second, they serve to make the head lighter, as they are largely filled with air rather than mass. If our sinuses were solid, they would add too much weight to an already heavy head and our slender necks would be further stressed. Third, they act as filters for dust, pollen, dirt, etc. When the filters get clogged, the sinuses act to remove the material by generating mucus. They also will fill up when the air is very dry to keep themselves from drying out.

HOME BURIAL

⊠⊠⊠

Q Somewhere I either heard of or read of a couple in Vermont that wrote a book about having your burial lot on your own property. I would love to get this book. Do you know about it?

E.P.M.
East Wallingford, Vermont

A There is a book called *Caring for Your Own Dead*, by Lias Carlson, published by Upper Publishers, P.O. Box 457, Hinesburg, VT 05461. B.W. of Barre, Vermont, wrote us, "Information required to handle home burial or cremation plans in all states is set out very specifically, so that Vermonters who wish to make their own arrangements, with little or no service from funeral home directors, are able to do so. A copy in paperback can be ordered for $14.95, postage paid."

CURLED PHOTOS

⊠⊠⊠

Q I have a boxful of old snapshots that are in curls. I have tried everything to straighten them out and to no avail. I would appreciate your help.

E.B.
Brandon, Vermont

A Our helpful friends at the New England Document Center in Andover, Massachusetts, said that what has made your snapshots curl is that the emulsion has dried at a faster rate than the printing paper. They suggest that you soak the photos until they flatten out, let them dry till damp, then lay them on blotting paper, cover with wax paper, and lay another layer of blotting paper on the top. Weight them down. You may have to do this twice. As soon as the photos are dry (i.e., not tacky), mount them immediately. NOTE: This process is not recommended for old carbon-process photos or those of real value; these should be handled by a trained conservator.

WOVEN NAMETAPES AND OLD USED CHRISTMAS CARDS

Q Can you tell me where I can order some woven nametapes for clothing? Also, I want the address for St. Jude's Ranch for Children. They asked for people to send them old used Christmas cards, but the address was on the TV screen such a short time, I couldn't get it down on paper.

E.E.B.
Rutland, Vermont

A Woven nametapes are available from Names Unlimited, P.O. Box 43821, Atlanta, GA 30378. Write and ask them to send you information. St. Jude's Ranch for Children's address is P.O. Box 8985, Boulder City, NV 89005-0985.

CRUSTY SCALES AROUND THE EYES

Q Please help. I'm desperate. I have rough skin and yellowish, crusty scales around my temples and under my eyes. Neither my doctor or dermatologist knows what they are or how to treat them. Could I have a vitamin deficiency? I use a soapless cleanser, rinse well, and I don't use creams.

DESPERATE in Rutland

A We suggested to Desperate that she see a nutritionist and/or holistic practitioner. The day after publication of our response we received the following letter. "A wacko response to Desperate in Rutland. Desperate is very likely to be suffering from a contact allergy to materials in his/her eyeglasses, goggle frames, or a surgical mask or some other article that contacts the undereye and temple areas of the skin. Metal spectacle frames are notorious offenders. Desperate should skip the nutritionist (really . . .) and make tracks to an allergist without delay."

Best Idea of the Week—Handy Sand

Fill one gallon plastic milk jugs with sand and keep some by the door and some in the car. The jugs are ideal for spreading the sand, especially if you get stuck. Thanks to D.W. of Stratford, Vermont, for telling us about this.

WINDCHILL FACTOR

✉✉✉✉✉✉✉✉✉✉✉✉✉✉✉✉✉✉✉✉✉✉✉✉✉✉✉✉✉✉✉✉✉✉✉✉✉

Q Before venturing to take your time with it, I posed this question to a couple of knowledgeable folk—who were not able to answer it. How is a windchill factor arrived at?

R.O.W.
Woodstock, Vermont

A We called one of our favorite weathermen, Stuart Hall, formerly with WCAX-TV in Burlington, Vermont. Stuart said the rule of thumb, which is very unsophisticated, is to take the wind speed, multiply it by 2, and subtract this figure from the temperature. The sophisticated system is too sophisticated for mere mortals to apply.

AUTOGRAPHS

✉✉✉✉✉✉✉✉✉✉✉✉✉✉✉✉✉✉✉✉✉✉✉✉✉✉✉✉✉✉✉✉✉✉✉✉✉

Q Could you put me in contact with autograph collectors? I have a notebook of twenty-one autographs which I've held on to since 1950. An uncle who was an electrician collected them for me when he worked on TV and Broadway shows. Some of the more famous include Jackie Gleason, Don Ameche, Frank Sinatra, Ginger Rogers, Groucho Marx, Jimmy Durante, and Eddie Cantor.

R.B.
Barre, Vermont

A We discovered two collectors' clubs where we think you could find the collectors that you're seeking: The Franklin Autograph Society, National Bank Building, 8 Broad Street, Hatfield, PA 19440, and Universal Autograph Collectors Club, P.O. Box 467, Rockville Center, NY 11571.

WALL STREET LEASE

Q I would be very grateful if you could help me. Everyone knows what and where Wall Street is. Well, Wall Street from the beginning was leased for ninety-nine years. Well, the ninety-nine years is up and the descendants of the man who leased it are in the process (or whatever they call it) of a lawsuit as the lease is up. The land was leased with no building on it. The name of the leaser is Rockwell. What I want to know is, could you tell me who to contact or where to write so I can find out if I am one of the descendants? According to my mother, I am, but I want to know for sure.

J.B.
Hardwick, Vermont

A We think you have things a little confused. In the 1930s the Rockefellers (not Rockwells) leased a tract of undeveloped land in midtown New York City for ninety-nine years and built Rockefeller Center on it. The ninety-nine years won't be up until the twenty-first century. There is no litigation by any heirs, because the land was leased from, and is still owned by, Columbia University. Wall Street is in one of the oldest parts of the city, and there were certainly buildings on it ninety-nine years ago! It is not owned by any one single individual or family, nor, to the best knowledge of the folks at the *New York Law Review* and the New York Real Estate Board, is there any litigation pending on any of the Wall Street properties.

MORMON GENEALOGICAL LIBRARY

Q I have been told that the Mormons have the largest genealogical library in the United States. However, no one seems to know the proper name or address. Would you be able to determine this information?

R.J.
Lake Bomoseen, Vermont

A You can write to The Family History Library of the Church of Jesus Christ of Latter-day Saints, 35 N.W. Temple, Salt Lake City, UT 84150, and request the genealogical information you need. Incidentally, the reason that the Mormons have been so active in the field of genealogy is that one of their three purposes on earth is to redeem the dead. They believe that baptism leads to salvation, but as there have been those in past history who did not have the opportunity to be baptized into the church, church members who are alive now work as their proxies, leading them through prayer into redemption.

STATIC ELECTRICITY

Q In the winter, on low-humidity days, I have a problem with static electricity. I work standing on a cement floor, and sparks fly when I hand something to others. I have tried using Static Guard, and it only lasts an hour or so. Is there any other way I can reduce this problem?

M.P.
Killington, Vermont

A We have two suggestions. The first is that you or your boss install a floor-model humidifier; this will take care of the low-humidity problem. The second, if the first is not feasible, is that you "ground" yourself by wearing rubber-soled shoes.

PRESERVING NEWSPAPER CLIPPINGS

Q My sister's photo was in the *New York Times*. I would like to preserve it. Is there any way, other than photocopying it, to do this?

NICK
Cambridge, Vermont

A The acid in the newspaper is what causes it to turn yellow and fall apart. Here's a concoction that removes the acidity from the paper: Dissolve a milk-ofmagnesia tablet in a quart of club soda overnight. Pour into a pan large enough to accommodate the flattened clipping. Paper is fragile when it's wet, so to prevent it from tearing, put a piece of nylon net in the pan beneath the clipping. Soak the clipping for up to one hour. Remove carefully and pat dry. Do not move until the paper is completely dry. Place a weight on top of the clipping once it's semidry to prevent its ends from curling.

CANCELED STAMPS

Q Is there a charitable organization that would accept canceled postage stamps?

M.B.
White River Junction, Vermont

A There are several organizations, our readers informed us. Koinonia Partners, Route 2, Americus, GA 31709, will take any commemorative stamps, stamps of denominations of $1 or over, and any and all foreign stamps. They sell them after soaking them off the envelope and request that you let *them* do this. Also, the Stamp Department, Vincentian Foreign Mission Society, Saint Mary's Seminary, Perryville, MO 63775 accepts any stamp of any denomination but asks donors not to send stamps that are torn, creased, stapled, clipped, or heavily canceled. Please leave a small margin of envelope around the stamp. Saint Albans Stamp Mission, P.O. Box Drawer 740, Ellenton, FL 34222, also seeks canceled stamps.

BABY SHOES BRONZED

✉✉

Q Could you find the address of a firm that bronzes baby shoes?

S.M.
Windsor, Vermont

A The American Bronzing Company, P.O. Box 6504, Bexley, OH 43209-9988, bronzes baby shoes. Write and ask for their catalogue.

REMOTE CONTROL INTERFERENCE

✉✉

Our good friend Mort Stillings wrote, "For the past few weeks I have been having problems with my remote control (hand-held) for my TV. It had been in the repair shop on two separate occasions, and there performed perfectly—bring it home and it was inoperative. It had several of us fellas scratching our heads! We finally pinned it down to an electrical field produced by the new "low-energy" high-wattage bulbs distributed by Green Mountain Power, which emit an electrical field when used near a TV and cancel out the infrared emission produced by hand-held remote control. If any of our friends are having this trouble, tell them to use this bulb at least 15 feet from the set, preferably in another room, and the problem will clear up very nicely all by itself!"

HOUSE FIRE AFTERMATH

There is a first-rate booklet called *After the Fire: Returning to Normal*. Herb Burkhard of Granville, New York, and member of the Penryhn Engine and Hose sent us a copy, and it includes pages of salvage hints that cover clothing, cooking utensils, electrical appliances, food, flooring, rugs, mattresses, books, locks, hinges, walls, and furniture. It's published by the U.S. Fire Administration, Federal Emergency Management Agency, Washington, DC 20472.

HOMEWORK

Q I answered an "Earn $ reading books" ad in our local paper. They need a fee of approximately $50, then they will send a packet of various materials outlining how to contact various companies who employ proofreaders, dust jacket writers, etc. Is this legitimate? They guarantee jobs or there is a money-back guarantee within the first year. What do you know about these ads?

P.B.
Barre, Vermont

A Our curiosity was sufficiently piqued by your letter and the ad you enclosed to lead us to call the telephone number in the ad. The person who answered asked us what extension we wanted (this company also advertises that you can make over $32,000 a year doing a variety of other things, like home assembly, watching TV, and stuffing envelopes ... but all in separate ads with different extensions) and when we told them, they asked if we had ever called before. When we said no, they said they could give us the information right then and there. They proceeded to reel off the information you had given us in your letter and then asked for our name, telephone number, and address. We asked why they wanted this information, and they replied, "So we can send you your packet" (for $50). "But we haven't made up our mind that we want it," we said. "We just want to clarify some of the information you've already given us." They hung up. We immediately dialed the Consumer Protection Division of the State Attorney General's Office and asked them if they knew about this operation. They told us that although they didn't know about this one specifically, it's typical of other similar scams proliferating around the country that involve offers of big bucks for working in your home. What are the scam warning signs? (1) If a company is asking you for money "up front" in order for you to be employed, watch out. Does McDonald's ask for a deposit or a sum to pay for a booklet on employee rules and benefits before they hire you? (2) Are they in fact hiring you or just sending you a list of people who *might* do so? (This kind of information, by the way, is publicly available if you are willing to do the research yourself.) (3) These people usually say there is a money-back guarantee. Don't believe them. Either there is something in small print that will invalidate the guarantee, or, even more likely, the company won't be around in a year. (4) Do not give them your name, address, or telephone number unless you know why they are asking for it. If you do, and they send you a package of unsolicited mail C.O.D., remember that you do not have to accept it. Finally, if you have any question about the legitimacy of any offer or "deal" made personally or through the mail, please contact your Attorney General's office. Their number is listed under State Government Services in the front of your phone book.

CREDIT CARD BONUS

Q From time to time I receive an appeal from a worthy organization, urging me to obtain a credit card in its name, which will entitle it to a financial bonus each time I make a purchase using that credit card. I would like to know how much of a financial bonus! A small fixed sum (how much?) each time I make a purchase? Or a small proportion (how small?) of the total of each purchase? No bank or organization I've contacted seems willing to divulge this information. Can you help?

N.C.
Benson, Vermont

A Good question! We started our research by calling Sally Budlong at the Vermont National Bank, and she connected us with the main branch's Customer Service Department. They explained that these cards are called affinity cards and that the Vermont National Bank has been offering them, in conjunction with several organizations, for about ten years. She explained that a portion of the total purchases is returned to the sponsoring organization. The percentage is negotiated with each group, and she wasn't able to divulge that information. Continuing the hunt for the elusive percentage of return, we learned that the Discover card returns 1 percent of the amount of purchases to the card owner each year; that Vermont ETV (Educational Television) offered an affinity card about two years ago through a Maryland bank and they received 1 percent of the cardholder's total purchases. They have discontinued this program because the administrative costs exceeded the amount they received. "Nightmare" was the word used to describe it by the fellow we spoke with at ETV's business office. We contacted the Vermont Council of the Arts; their fiscal officer said the affinity card program was just going into place and their organization would receive ½ of 1 percent of the total purchases. So there you have it: a long-winded reply with rebates running from ½ of 1 percent to 1 percent in this neck of the woods.

N.B. of Barre, Vermont, sent us this suggestion: "The Discover card put out by Sears is available at no initial charge—and no annual charges—wholly free. A person could take the 1 percent Discover refund each year and add that to the normal annual charge for other cards (which they would no longer use) and give it to any organization of their choice." And if the organization is a charitable one, they even get to take a tax deduction!

A Springfield resident wrote us to let us know that the Discover card is no longer free. "I received my card and a bill for one year for $9.00. Still a good value as other cards charge more; also, one gets a bonus at the end of the year."

READER FEEDBACK

SOFT DRINK SWITCH

🖂🖂

Q The Burger King chain has switched from Pepsi to Coca-Cola. Why did this happen?

P.P., PEPSI FAN
Waterbury Village, Vermont

A To better answer your question, we called Customer Service at Burger King's headquarters in Miami. We were told the following: "Burger King switched to Coke because of its better ability to provide a powerful mix of brand drink, technology, and distinctive brand of service." We asked the lady with whom we were speaking to please repeat the above, as it didn't make a whole lot of sense to us. She repeated it. We then asked if it made any sense to her. "Not a whole lot," she replied, "but that's all we've been given." Finding the official explanation unsatisfactory, to say the least, we hurried down to our local library and looked up Burger King in *Standard & Poor's Registry*. We discovered that it is a subsidiary of the Pillsbury Corporation, which is in turn owned by a British holding company called Grand Metropolitan, which is based in London, England. We were reluctant to make a transatlantic call, so instead got in touch with a stockbroker friend of ours. He remembered reading about the switch. "So why did they do it?" we asked. "The bottom line . . . profit," he replied. "Coke undersold Pepsi: Burger King went with the low bid." So if you want a Pepsi with your meal, you'll have to go to Pizza Hut. The chain is owned by Pepsico.

BIRTHDAY CARD FROM THE PRESIDENT

Q I would like an address for the White House. I saw it somewhere, maybe in your column, but can't locate it now. I would like to have birthday cards sent from the President.

A RUPERT READER

A The Greeting Office at the White House will send birthday cards, signed by the President, to people age eighty or older and to couples celebrating their fiftieth anniversary or beyond. The cards must be requested three months in advance of the date. The address is: Attn: Greeting Office, The White House, Office of Communications, Washington, DC 20500.

HUMPS IN RUG

Q I have a problem which I hope you can help me solve. I have a 12′ × 24′ unpatterned wool living room carpet, on a pad, not wall to wall. It has two persistent, rather prominent ridges and some smaller ones which will not flatten out with hand stretching or weighting. They become more pronounced in humid weather. The perimeter of the carpet is even and smooth and is kept taut by furniture upon it. I do not wish to nail the carpet to the pine floor. Is there any treatment that would smooth the affected portion? The "humps" appeared some years ago after young folk wrestled on the middle of the carpet.

M.M.R.
Rutland, Vermont

A If the rug was folded over by the wrestlers, it could have put a permanent crease in it. If the backing on the rug is sisal or jute, the humps can be steamed out. Turn the carpet over and use a damp towel and iron or hand steamer. It's imperative that you allow the carpet to dry thoroughly and then turn it right side up. If the pad is in more than one piece, it may have shifted or gotten bunched up, which could also be causing humps.

CONSIGNMENT FEES

Q When putting homemade items in a store on consignment, what percentage of the sale goes to the consignee?

WONDERING
Wallingford, Vermont

A The rule of thumb is that 40 percent of the retail price goes to the consignee (i.e., the store in which you have placed your items) and 60 percent goes to you.

HOW LONG TO KEEP HOSPITAL RECORDS

Q I am writing to ask help in finding out exactly what papers or records should be kept after hospital visits stop and all payments are made. They accumulate because we have to make copies for our insurance company. One ends up with a huge folder full of records. My feeling is that one should keep only the records of tests already given, CAT scans, and X rays. Please help.

J.K.
Woodsville, N.H.

A The only records that you need to keep are the ones used for tax purposes. (All tax-related information should be kept for seven years.) Copies of reports, tests, scans, etc., are sent to your doctor and kept in your file.

RICE FOR DOGS

When one of Nan's geriatric dogs went off her feed, we were stumped, but Nan's friend Doris Cole suggested we cook up some rice and pour a little fat over it. We used bacon grease and brown rice, and Nan's dog Ginny licked her bowl clean. We've also used rice when we discover there's no dog food and no one wants to go to town to get some.

SOURCES AND SUPPLIERS

INDEX

SOURCES AND SUPPLIERS

Acme Book Binding
100 Cambridge Street
Charlestown, MA 02129

Allied Plastics
925 Orchard Lake Road
Pontiac, MI 48053

Amazon Drygoods
2218 East 11th Street
Davenport, IA 52803-3760

American Bronzing Company
P.O. Box 6504
Bexley, OH 43209-9988

G. G. Bean
Box 638
Brunswick, ME 04011

Beer and Wine Hobby
P.O. Box M
Melrose, MA 02176
tel. (617) 665-8442

J. C. Boardman Company
Hartford Turnpike South
Wallingford, CT 06492

Braid-Aid
466 Washington Street
Pembroke, MA 02359

Bryant Stove Works
Thorndike, ME 04986
tel. (207) 568-3663

Cheyenne Outfitters
tel. 1-800-234-0432

Cinderella of Boston, Inc.
P.O. Box 71100
Canoga Park, CA 91304

The Clothes Press
P.O. Box 686
Montpelier, VT 05601-0686

Collector Books
P.O. Box 3009
Paducah, KY 42001

The Company Store
2809 Losey Boulevard
La Crosse, WI 54601
tel. 1-800-356-9367

Milton and Mary Corey
R#2, Box 432
Chester, VT 05143

Craft Patterns Studio
3N345 North 12th Street
St. Charles, IL 60174

"Crib Safety: Keep Them on the Safe Side"
Product Safety Fact Sheet No. 43
U.S. Consumer Product Safety
    Commission
Washington, DC 20207

Diamond Brands Inc.
Customer Service
1804 Cloquet Avenue
Cloquet, MN 55720

Direct Marketing Association
11 West 42nd Street
New York, NY 10036

Down Under Company
Route 100
Weston, VT 05160

Easi-Bild Pattern Company
Box 2383-15241
Pleasantville, NY 10570

Endosome Biological Company
Williamsville, NY 14221

Dave Erickson
P.O. Box 2275
Littleton, MA 01460

Essex Umbrella Manufacturing Company
145 Old Colony Avenue
Quincy, MA 02170
tel. (617) 770-2707

The Family History Library of the Church of Jesus Christ of Latter-day Saints
35 N.W. Temple
Salt Lake City, UT 84150

The Franklin Autograph Society
National Bank Building
8 Broad Street
Hatfield, PA 19440

David Freiberg
Cerebro Lithographers
Box 1221
Lancaster, PA 17603

Gardener's Supply
128 Intervale Road
Burlington, VT 05401
tel. (802) 863-1700

Gawett Marble and Granite
Center Rutland, VT 05736

Graceland
Communications Department
P.O. Box 16508
Memphis, TN 03816-0508

Green Mountain Spinnery
Box 568
Putney, VT 05346
tel. 1-800-321-9665

Attn: Greeting Office
The White House
Office of Communications
Washington, DC 20500

Grinling, Ltd.
192 Christopher Columbus Drive
Jersey City, NJ 07302

"Tobacco Bill" Hatcher
713 Parrott Avenue
Kingston, NC 28501

Hill Brothers
99 Ninth Street
Lynchburg, VA 24504

Home-Sew
Bethlehem, PA 18018

Rita Howell
4000 Greenwood Boulevard
Harrisburg, PA 17109

**Institute of Certified Financial
Planners**
10065 East Harvard Avenue
Denver, CO 80231

International Friendship League
22 Batterymarch Street
Boston, MA 02109

**International Seal, Label and
Cigar Band Society**
1985 East Bellevue Street
Tucson, AZ 85715

Journal Graphics
269 Broadway
New York, NY 10007
tel. (212) 227-7323

Koinonia Partners
Route 2
Americus, GA 31709

Lehman Hardware and Appliances
P.O. Box 41
Kidron, OH 44636

Neville Lewis
HCR 68, Box 130L
Cushing, ME 04563
tel. (207) 354-8055

Luce Corporation
336 Putnam Avenue
P.O. Box 4124
Hamden, CT 06514

Luther Ford and Company
Box 201405
Bloomington, MN 55420

Macy's Texas Stove Works
5515 Alameda Road
Houston, TX 77004

Mantis Manufacturing Company
1458 County Line Road
Department 775
Huntingdon Valley, PA 19006

The Maytag Company
Newton, IA 50208
tel. (515) 792-7000

Midwest Antique Stove Information, Clearing House and Parts Registry
417 North Main Street
Monticello, IN 47960

***Mushroom Growing*, No. A2760**
Agricultural Bulletin Building
1535 Observatory Drive
Madison, WI 53706

Names Unlimited
P.O. Box 43821
Atlanta, GA 30378

National Button Society
2733 Juno Place
Akron, OH 44333

National Mail Order Center
The Sperry and Hutchinson
   Company, Inc.
P.O. Box 5775
Norcross, GA 30091
tel. 1-800-874-4438

Newark Dressmakers Supply
6473 Ruch Road
P.O. Box 20730
Lehigh Valley, PA 18002-0730

New Horizons
Joann Champion
P.O. Box 769
Andover Road
Chester, VT 05143

Occupied Japan Club
c/o Florence Archambault
29 Freedom Street
Newport, RI 02840

Orum Silver Company
P.O. Box 805
51 South Vine Street
Meriden, CT 06450

Past Patterns
P.O. Box 7587
Grand Rapids, MI 49510

P. L. Premium Leather by Hanover
P.O. Box 340
Hanover, PA 17331

Regal Cookware
Attn: Consumer Service
1675 Reigle Drive
Kewaskum, WI 53040

Kenneth Rendell
154 Wells Avenue
Newton, MA 02159
tel. 1-800-447-1007

The Resolution Trust Corporation
550 17th Street N.W.
Washington, DC 20429
tel. (202) 789-6313

Re-Tinning and Copper Repair
525 West 26th Street
New York, NY 10001
tel. (212) 244-4896

Revere Ware
Customer Service
P.O. Box 250
Clinton, IL 16127

Rutland Products
tel. 1-800-222-6340;
   1-800-544-1307

Saint Albans Stamp Mission
P.O. Box Drawer 740
Ellenton, FL 34222

St. Jude's Ranch for Children
P.O. Box 8985
Boulder City, NV 89005-0985

Seventh Generation
Burlington, VT
tel. 1-800-456-1177

Sheplers
Wichita, KS
tel. 1-800-833-7007

The Shop of William Farwell
RR #229
Chittenden, VT 05737

Student Letter Exchange
215 Fifth Avenue S.E.
Waseca, MN 56093

Taunton Press
63 South Main Street
P.O. Box 5506
Newton, CT 06470-5506

The Tinning Company
69 Norman Street
Everett, MA 02149
tel. (617) 389-3400

U.S. Fire Administration
Federal Emergency Management
   Agency
Washington, DC 20472

**Universal Autograph Collectors
Club**
P.O. Box 467
Rockville Center, NY 11571

University Products, Inc.
P.O. Box 101
Holyoke, MA 01401

Upper Publishers
P.O. Box 457
Hinesburg, VT 05461

Vermont Country Store
P.O. Box 3000
Manchester Center, VT 05255-3000
tel. (802) 362-2400

**Vermont Statehood Bicentennial
Commission**
P.O. Box 6833
Rutland, VT 05702

**Vincentian Foreign Mission
Society**
Stamp Department
Saint Mary's Seminary
Perryville, MO 63775

We love to get mail from our readers—both questions for us to
answer in future books, and reader feedback on subjects we've
discussed in this one. Please write to us at:

Anne and Nan
P.O. Box 210
Hartland, VT 05048

INDEX

2T Clorox : 1 pt water in a spray bottle